Echoes of Wisdom

World's Most Famous Quotes Explained

Author   Catalin Ladaru

Contents

Echoes of Wisdom

World's Most Famous Quotes Explained

Welcome!

Every day we hear different quotes from different people associating them with different actions. It is time to fully understand those quotes and engrave them in our minds.

In the tapestry of human expression, certain phrases have transcended their original contexts to become landmarks of collective wisdom and insight. This book ventures into the heart of these enduring words, unpacking the layers of meaning and the historical backdrops against which they were first uttered. This book is not just a collection, it is an exploration into the psyche of humanity, a journey through the thoughts and moments that have shaped our world.

Through its pages, readers will be tracing the origins of quotes that have become cornerstones of cultural lexicon. From ancient philosophers to modern-day leaders, from poets to scientists, and activists to artists, this book spans a diverse range of voices who had an impact on our society.

"Echoes of Wisdom" aims to do more than just recount these famous words; it seeks to offer a deeper understanding of their significance. Why did these phrases resonate so widely? What can they tell us about the human condition, societal values, and the ever-evolving nature of language and communication?

This book invites readers on an enlightening journey—a chance to rediscover the most quoted words in history, to uncover the wisdom, pain, joy, and irony they encapsulate. It is an opportunity to see the world through the eyes of those who have left an indelible mark on it with their words. Whether you are a lover of history, a seeker of knowledge, or simply someone who appreciates the power of words, ""Echoes of Wisdom " promises to enrich your understanding of these iconic utterances and offer a new perspective on the world.

Join us as we delve into the stories behind the quotes, revealing the human experiences and universal truths they embody. This creation is more than just a book, it is a testament to the enduring power of language to inspire, to challenge, and to connect us across time and space.

Chapter1. General quotes

Each of these quotes encapsulates a profound truth about life, ambition, perseverance, and the human spirit. They remind us that with the right mindset, resilience, and determination, achieving our dreams and overcoming obstacles is possible.

1."I think, therefore I am." - René Descartes

This foundational statement of Western philosophy was penned by René Descartes in the 17th century. It suggests that the very act of thinking proves one's existence. Descartes sought a statement that could be beyond all doubt, arriving at the conclusion that if he doubted, there must be a thinking mind to do the doubting. Hence, his existence was undeniable.

2. "To be, or not to be, that is the question." - William Shakespeare

From Shakespeare's play "Hamlet," this quote reflects the protagonist's existential crisis and contemplation of life and death. Hamlet muses on the nature of existence and whether it is better to live, enduring life's hardships, or to die, escaping to something worse or unknown.

3."The only thing we have to fear is fear itself." - Franklin D. Roosevelt

Spoken by Roosevelt during his inaugural address in 1933, amidst the Great Depression, this quote aimed to rally the American people. It emphasizes that fear, particularly the fear of economic collapse, was worsening the nation's plight and that courage and resolve were necessary for recovery.

4."In the end, we will remember not the words of our enemies, but the silence of our friends." - Martin Luther King Jr.

This quote from civil rights leader Martin Luther King Jr. highlights the importance of support and advocacy. It suggests that betrayal or hurt from those we consider allies, through their inaction or silence on critical issues, impacts us more deeply than the actions of those openly against us.

William Shakespeare was an English playwright, poet, and actor. He is widely regarded as the greatest writer in the English language and the world's pre-eminent dramatist. He is often called England's national poet and the "Bard of Avon".

Born: April 1564, Stratford-upon-Avon, United Kingdom
Died: April 23, 1616 (age 52 years)

5."All men are created equal." - Declaration of Independence, USA

A cornerstone of American democratic ideals, this quote from the Declaration of Independence asserts that every individual has inherent value and rights. It is a principle that challenges injustices like slavery and discrimination, advocating for equality before the law.

6."Give me liberty or give me death!" - Patrick Henry

A declaration made by Patrick Henry in 1775 to the Virginia Convention, calling for armed resistance against British rule. It embodies the American spirit of valuing freedom more than anything else, even life itself, and played a significant role in rallying support for the American Revolution.

7."I have a dream." - Martin Luther King Jr.

Part of a historic speech delivered during the 1963 March on Washington, King outlined his vision of an America free from racial discrimination. This quote, and the speech, became symbolic of the civil rights movement and its aspirations for equality and justice.

8."That's one small step for man, one giant leap for mankind." - Neil Armstrong

Spoken by astronaut Neil Armstrong as he became the first person to step onto the moon in 1969. This quote captures the monumental significance of the Apollo 11 mission, not just as a technological achievement but as a milestone for human exploration and potential.

9."To be yourself in a world that is constantly trying to make you something else is the greatest accomplishment." - Ralph Waldo Emerson

Emerson, an American essayist, and philosopher, emphasizes the value of individuality and the courage it takes to maintain one's own identity in the face of societal pressures and expectations.

Martin Luther King Jr. was an American Christian minister, activist, and political philosopher who was one of the most prominent leaders in the civil rights movement from 1955 until his assassination in 1968.

Born: January 15, 1929, Atlanta, GA
Assassinated: April 4, 1968

10."For every minute you are angry you lose sixty seconds of happiness." - Ralph Waldo Emerson

This quote reminds us of the fleeting nature of life and the futility of spending it in anger or resentment. Emerson advocates for a positive outlook, suggesting that happiness is a choice obscured by negative emotions.

11."Two things are infinite: the universe and human stupidity; and I'm not sure about the universe." - Albert Einstein

Often attributed to Einstein, this humorous quote reflects on the boundless nature of human folly compared to the mysteries of the universe. It is a wry observation of the human condition and our capacity for irrationality.

12."It is never too late to be what you might have been." - George Eliot

George Eliot (the pen name of Mary Ann Evans) offers encouragement and hope with this quote. It suggests that personal growth and change are always possible, regardless of past actions or current circumstances.

13."The future belongs to those who believe in the beauty of their dreams." - Eleanor Roosevelt

This quote from the former First Lady and human rights advocate encourages optimism and perseverance. Roosevelt emphasizes that a strong belief in one's ideals and aspirations is foundational to achieving success and shaping the future.

**14."You must be the change you wish to see in the world."
- Gandhi**

This powerful statement encapsulates Gandhi's philosophy of personal responsibility and active participation in societal change. It is a call to action, urging individuals to embody the virtues and values they hope to promote within society. Gandhi believed that meaningful change begins with the individual. The quote suggests that before we can change the world, we must first change ourselves. This change could be in terms of our attitudes, our actions, or our approach to dealing with problems. Gandhi's own life was a testament to living one's principles—his commitment to truth, nonviolence, and simplicity was evident in his personal and public life.

Mohandas Karamchand Gandhi was an Indian lawyer, anti-colonial nationalist and political ethicist who employed nonviolent resistance to lead the successful campaign for India's independence from British rule. He inspired movements for civil rights and freedom across the world.

Born: October 2, 1869, Porbandar, India
Assassinated: January 30, 1948

Chapter 2. Wealth quotes

Each of these quotes encapsulates distinct perspectives on wealth, from philosophical insights to practical advice, offering a multifaceted understanding of what it means to be truly wealthy.

1.Making the first million is hard, making the next 100 million is easy. - Unknown

The quote encapsulates a widely recognized truth about wealth accumulation and financial success. While the statement is often attributed to various successful individuals, including oil magnate John D. Rockefeller, its core message remains consistent: the initial phase of earning or saving to reach a significant financial milestone like one million dollars poses the greatest challenge. Here are several reasons why this saying holds weight:

-*Starting from Scratch*: For most people, the journey to their first million involves starting with little to no capital. This means that every dollar towards that first million often requires direct labor and effort, unlike subsequent millions that can be earned through investments, interest, or leveraging existing assets.

-*Learning Curve*: Achieving significant financial success usually requires knowledge and skills that take time to develop. Mistakes made early on can be costly, but they are also invaluable learning experiences. Once an individual has navigated the complexities of their financial landscape to make their first million, they are better equipped to use those lessons to earn more efficiently moving forward.

-Compound Interest: In the context of investments, the principle of compound interest means that your money earns interest, and then that interest earns interest on itself. The effects of compounding are modest at first but grow exponentially over time. Thus, building the initial capital takes time and patience, after which the growth of wealth can accelerate.

-*Risk Management*: The path to the first million often involves understanding and managing risks. Early in one's financial journey, the tolerance for risk might be lower because there's more to lose relative to one's net worth. As wealth grows, individuals can often afford to take calculated risks, which can lead to higher returns.

-*Psychological Barriers*: There is also a psychological aspect to achieving this milestone. The goal of earning a million dollars can seem daunting and unreachable from the outset. Overcoming self-doubt and maintaining motivation amidst challenges and setbacks is a significant part of the journey.

-Economies of Scale: In business, the concept of economies of scale can apply to wealth accumulation. As investments grow larger, opportunities for more significant and diverse investments open up, which can lead to higher returns. The initial phase of accumulating wealth doesn't benefit as much from these economies of scale.

Once the first million is achieved, the experience, knowledge, confidence, and financial principles learned along the way can make it easier to earn subsequent millions. The initial milestone also often provides the capital necessary to make larger, more lucrative investments or business decisions, further accelerating wealth accumulation.

2. The quickest way to double your money is to fold it in half and put it back in your pocket." - Will Rogers

This humorous quote serves as a caution against the allure of get-rich-quick schemes and the risks of speculative investing. Rogers reminds us of the value of prudence and saving, suggesting that sometimes the best financial strategy is to avoid unnecessary spending and to safeguard what one already has.

3. "Do not save what is left after spending but spend what is left after saving." - Warren Buffett

Buffett's advice shifts the conventional approach to managing money, advocating for prioritizing savings over spending. This principle encourages financial discipline, ensuring that individuals build a safety net and invest in their future before indulging in non-essential expenditures, which is a foundational strategy for wealth accumulation.

4. "When you play the game of thrones, you win, or you die. There is no middle ground." - George R.R. Martin

Although this quote from a fictional context might not directly address financial wealth, it metaphorically speaks to the high stakes and ruthless nature of pursuits for power and success. It can be interpreted as a commentary on the competitive nature of business and the risks involved in striving for the top, emphasizing the need for total commitment and the dangers of half-measures.

5. "Rich people have small TVs and big libraries, and poor people have small libraries and big TVs." - Zig Ziglar

This observation by Ziglar contrasts the spending habits and priorities of the wealthy versus the less affluent. It suggests that investing in personal development, education, and continuous learning is a common trait among the wealthy, implying that such investments contribute more to lasting wealth than spending on transient pleasures.

6. "An investment in knowledge pays the best interest." - Benjamin Franklin

Franklin highlights the unparalleled value of education and continuous learning. Unlike material investments that can depreciate or become obsolete, knowledge accumulates and appreciates over time, providing ongoing dividends in the form of better decision-making, innovation, and the ability to navigate the complexities of the world.

7. "The stock market is filled with individuals who know the price of everything, but the value of nothing." - Philip Fisher

Fisher criticizes the short-term, speculative approach to investing, where decisions are made based on price movements rather than understanding the intrinsic value of assets. This quote champions the philosophy of value investing, which focuses on long-term fundamentals rather than short-term market fluctuations.

8. "Money is a terrible master but an excellent servant." - P.T. Barnum

This quote reflects on the dual nature of money. When one becomes obsessed with accumulating wealth, it can lead to a life dominated by the pursuit of money, which can be unsatisfying and destructive. However, when money is used wisely as a tool to achieve goals, support worthwhile causes, and improve one's life and the lives of others, it serves a valuable and positive purpose.

Benjamin Franklin was an American polymath, a leading writer, scientist, inventor, statesman, diplomat, printer, publisher, and political philosopher.

He is best known as the only Founding Father who signed all three documents that freed America from Britain. Franklin is credited with drafting the Declaration of Independence and the American Constitution.

Born: January 17, 1706, Milk Street, Boston, MA
Died: April 17, 1790

9."It's not the employer who pays the wages. Employers only handle the money. It's the customer who pays the wages." - Henry Ford

Ford's statement underscores the importance of the customer in any business equation. It highlights the fact that the sustainability of a business, and thus the wealth it generates for its owners and employees, is ultimately dependent on its ability to meet customer needs and demands. This quote is a reminder of the foundational role of value creation in wealth generation.

10. "Wealth consists not in having great possessions, but in having few wants." – Epictetus

Coming from a Stoic philosopher, this quote emphasizes contentment and simplicity. It posits that true wealth is achieved not by accumulating more but by desiring less. This perspective encourages a reevaluation of what is genuinely necessary for happiness and fulfillment, highlighting that freedom from material desires leads to true abundance.

11. "The real measure of your wealth is how much you'd be worth if you lost all your money." – Unknown

This quote challenges the conventional measure of wealth that focuses solely on financial assets. It suggests that true wealth encompasses intangible assets such as skills, knowledge, relationships, and character. The essence of this quote lies in understanding that one's value is not diminished by the loss of material possessions.

Henry Ford was an American industrialist and business magnate. As founder of the Ford Motor Company, he is credited as a pioneer in making automobiles affordable for middle-class Americans through the Fordism system.

Born: July 30, 1863, Springwell Township, Michigan
Died: April 7, 1947

Chapter 3. Health quotes

Each quote sheds light on distinct aspects of health, from the importance of preventive care and physical fitness to the intrinsic value of health over material wealth. Together, they offer a comprehensive view of health as a multifaceted and invaluable aspect of life.

1."Health is wealth." – Unknown

This quote draws a direct comparison between health and wealth, emphasizing that good health is the most valuable asset one can possess. It suggests that without health, material wealth has little value, underlining the importance of prioritizing health above all else.

2. "Let food be thy medicine and medicine be thy food." – Hippocrates

Hippocrates, often considered the father of medicine, advocated for the healing power of diet. This quote suggests that what we eat directly impacts our health, proposing a preventive approach to healthcare where nutrition is key to preventing and treating illness.

3. "To keep the body in good health is a duty... otherwise we shall not be able to keep our mind strong and clear." – Buddha

Buddha's words highlight the interconnectedness of physical and mental health. By suggesting it's our duty to maintain our bodies, it implies that physical health is essential for mental clarity and strength, emphasizing a holistic view of well-being.

4. "Physical fitness is the first requisite of happiness." - Joseph Pilates

Joseph Pilates places physical fitness as the cornerstone of happiness, suggesting that being in good physical condition is fundamental to experiencing joy and satisfaction in life. This underscores the role of fitness in enhancing quality of life.

Siddhartha Gautama, most referred to as the Buddha, was a wandering ascetic and religious teacher who lived in South Asia during the 6th or 5th century BCE and founded Buddhism.

Born: Lumbini, Lumbini Sanskritik, Nepal
Died: Kushinagar, India

5. "Health is not valued until sickness comes." - Thomas Fuller

Fuller's quote serves as a reminder that people often take their health for granted and only realize its importance when they become ill.

This statement is a call to appreciate and prioritize health before it's compromised.

6. "He who has health has hope; and he who has hope has everything." - Arabian Proverb

This proverb links health with hope, suggesting that good health is a source of optimism and possibility. It conveys the idea that health is a foundational element that enables us to pursue our goals and dreams.

7. "It is health that is real wealth and not pieces of gold and silver." - Mahatma Gandhi

Gandhi's quote criticizes materialism and underscores the superior value of health over monetary wealth. It suggests that true richness comes from being healthy, as without health, material riches have little significance.

8. "Wellness encompasses a healthy body, a sound mind, and a tranquil spirit. Enjoy the journey as you strive for wellness." - Laurette Gagnon Beaulieu

Beaulieu emphasizes wellness as a holistic concept that includes physical health, mental well-being, and spiritual peace. The quote encourages us to find joy in the ongoing process of maintaining and improving our overall health.

9. "Early to bed and early to rise, makes a man healthy, wealthy, and wise." - Benjamin Franklin

Franklin's adage suggests that simple daily habits, such as getting enough sleep and starting the day early, contribute significantly to one's health, prosperity, and wisdom. It highlights the importance of discipline and routine in achieving a balanced and fulfilling life.

10. "The greatest wealth is health." – Virgil

Virgil reinforces the idea that the truest form of wealth is not found in material possessions but in maintaining good health. This ancient wisdom highlights the timeless value of health as foundational to life's enjoyment and fulfillment.

Thomas Fuller, also known as "Negro Demus" and the "Virginia Calculator", was an enslaved African renowned for his mathematical abilities.

Born: 1710, Benin , West Africa **, Died:** 1790

Chapter 4. Success quotes

Together, these quotes present a multifaceted view of success, emphasizing hard work, resilience, passion, and the importance of making a positive impact as key elements in achieving true success.

1. "Success is not the key to happiness. Happiness is the key to success. If you love what you are doing, you will be successful." - Albert Schweitzer

Schweitzer suggests that success should not be pursued for its own sake or as a means to achieve happiness. Instead, happiness itself, derived from passion and fulfillment in one's endeavors, naturally leads to success. The quote underscores the importance of aligning one's work with their passions and interests as the foundation for true success.

2. "Success is the ability to go from one failure to another with no loss of enthusiasm." - Winston Churchill

Churchill highlights resilience and perseverance as crucial components of success. The journey to success is often paved with failures, and the ability to maintain enthusiasm and optimism through these challenges is what ultimately leads to achievement. This quote reminds us that success is as much about the journey and how we handle setbacks as it is about the outcome.

3. "The only place where success comes before work is in the dictionary." - Vidal Sassoon

Sassoon's witty observation points out that success is the result of hard work and effort, not luck or entitlement. The quote is a call to action, emphasizing that achievement is earned through dedication and perseverance, debunking any myths of shortcuts to success.

Former Prime Minister of the United Kingdom

Born: November 30, 1874, Blenheim Palace, United Kingdom

Died: January 24, 1965

4. "Success is not final, failure is not fatal: It is the courage to continue that counts." - Winston Churchill

Another powerful quote from Churchill, it serves as a reminder that neither success nor failure is absolute. Success should not lead to complacency, and failure should not deter one from pursuing their goals. The essence of true success lies in the courage to persist and continue striving despite obstacles.

5. "Success is not how high you have climbed, but how you make a positive difference to the world." - Roy T. Bennett

Bennett shifts the focus from personal achievement and status to the impact one has on others and the world. This quote redefines success as the ability to contribute positively and make a difference, suggesting that true success is measured by the value one adds to the lives of others and society as a whole.

6. "Success usually comes to those who are too busy to be looking for it." - Henry David Thoreau

Thoreau suggests that success is a byproduct of hard work and dedication to one's pursuits. By focusing on the work and putting in the effort, success naturally follows. This quote encourages a focus on the process rather than the outcome, implying that those fully immersed in their endeavors are more likely to achieve success.

7. "To succeed in life, you need two things: ignorance and confidence." - Mark Twain

Twain's quote humorously posits that success requires a blend of confidence and a certain level of ignorance, or perhaps a better term might be 'naiveté.' The idea is that being unaware of the supposed limits and obstacles can free individuals to pursue their goals with confidence, often leading to success that might have seemed unlikely from a conventional standpoint.

8. " "The secret of success is to do the common thing uncommonly well." - John D. Rockefeller Jr.

Rockefeller Jr. points to excellence in even the most mundane tasks as a key to success. By excelling in the basics and executing with exceptional quality, one can stand out and achieve success. This quote highlights the value of diligence, attention to detail, and the pursuit of quality in all endeavors.

9. "I have failed again and again throughout my life. That's why I've been successful." - Michael Jordan

Michael Jordan, one of the greatest basketball players of all time, attributes his success to his many failures. This quote underscores the invaluable lessons learned through failure and how they can pave the way to success. It highlights the importance of resilience, learning from mistakes, and using failure as a steppingstone to greatness.

Michael Jeffrey Jordan, also known by his initials MJ, is an American businessman and former professional basketball player. He played fifteen seasons in the National Basketball Association between 1984 and 2003, winning six NBA championships with the Chicago Bulls.

Born: February 17, 1963 ,Cumberland Hospital

Chapter 5. Motivational quotes

Motivational quotes have the power to inspire action, ignite passion, and remind us of our potential. Each of these quotes encapsulates the truth about the human spirit, resilience, and the pursuit of excellence. Let them serve as reminders that, no matter where you are on your journey, the potential for greatness lies within your grasp.

1."Whether you think you can, or you think you can't – you're right." - Henry Ford

Ford's words highlight the power of mindset. If you believe in your ability to succeed, that confidence will help make it a reality. Conversely, doubt can lead to failure.

2. "It does not matter how slowly you go as long as you do not stop." – Confucius

The emphasis here is on the importance of continuous effort over speed. Making steady progress, no matter how slow, is better than rushing or giving up.

3. "The best time to plant a tree was 20 years ago. The second-best time is now." - Chinese Proverb

This proverb encourages us to start working towards our goals now, rather than regretting not starting earlier. It's a call to action, reminding us that the best time to begin is always the present.

4. "Hardships often prepare ordinary people for an extraordinary destiny." - C.S. Lewis

Lewis suggests that difficulties and challenges can prepare us for something greater. Our struggles can lead to significant personal growth and eventual success.

Confucius, born Kong Qiu was a Chinese philosopher of the Spring and Autumn period who is traditionally considered the paragon of Chinese sages. Confucius's teachings and philosophy underpin the East Asian culture and society and remain influential across China and East Asia to this day.

Born: Qufu, Jining, China

5. "It's not whether you get knocked down, it's whether you get up." - Vince Lombardi

Lombardi highlights the importance of getting back up after a fall. Success isn't about never failing but about how we respond to failure.

6. "You are never too old to set another goal or to dream a new dream." - C.S. Lewis

This quote encourages us never to stop setting new goals or dreaming new dreams, regardless of age. It's a reminder that growth and ambition have no expiration date.

**7. "Don't watch the clock; do what it does. Keep going."
- Sam Levenson**

Levenson's advice is to emulate the clock's relentless progress by continuously moving forward, emphasizing the value of perseverance and constant effort.

8. Everything you've ever wanted is on the other side of fear."   - George Addair

This quote suggests that achieving our desires often requires us to confront and overcome our fears. The rewards we seek lie beyond the barriers of fear.

9. "Opportunities don't happen, you create them." - Chris Grosser

Grosser challenges the notion that opportunities simply happen. Instead, he argues that through initiative and effort, we can create our own chances for success.

10. "Don't be pushed around by the fears in your mind. Be led by the dreams in your heart." - Roy T. Bennett

Bennett advises us to be guided by our aspirations and passions rather than our fears, emphasizing the power of positive motivation over negative influences.

Jimmy Dean Foods is an American brand of meat products marketed and owned by Tyson Foods. The company was founded in 1969 by country singer and actor Jimmy Dean. It was purchased by Sara Lee, which then divested as part of a unit known as Hillshire Brands, which was later purchased by Tyson Foods.

11. "I can't change the direction of the wind, but I can adjust my sails to always reach my destination." - Jimmy Dean

Dean's quote is about the importance of being flexible and adaptable in the face of challenges. It's not about the obstacles but how we respond to them that matters.

12. "Your time is limited, don't waste it living someone else's life." - Steve Jobs

Jobs warns against the trap of living according to others' expectations. He champions authenticity and the pursuit of one's own path as the essence of a meaningful life.

13. "Do what you can with all you have, wherever you are." - Theodore Roosevelt

This quote is about resourcefulness—using whatever resources you have at your disposal, wherever you are, to move forward.

14. "Strive not to be a success, but rather to be of value." - Albert Einstein

Einstein suggests that the pursuit of success for its own sake is less important than striving to be valuable—to contribute something meaningful to the world.

Albert Einstein was a German-born theoretical physicist who is widely held to be one of the greatest and most influential scientists of all time.
Born: March 14, 1879, Ulm, Germany
Died: April 18, 1955

Theodore Roosevelt Jr., often referred to as Teddy or by his initials, T. R., was an American politician, statesman, conservationist, naturalist, and writer who served as the 26th president of the United States from 1901 to 1909.

Born: October 27, 1858, Theodore Roosevelt Birthplace National Historic Site, New York, NY
Died: January 6, 1919

Chapter 6. Life quotes

Each of these quotes offers a unique perspective on how to live life fully and meaningfully, emphasizing the importance of learning, giving, embracing the present, and forging our own paths. They inspire us to consider what it means to live well, beyond mere survival or routine existence, urging us toward a life of purpose and growth.

1."Live as if you were to die tomorrow. Learn as if you were to live forever." - Mahatma Gandhi

Gandhi's quote encourages us to embrace each day with urgency and passion as if it were our last, appreciating the present and making the most of now. Simultaneously, it advocates for a lifelong pursuit of knowledge and growth, suggesting that the thirst for learning should never cease, as if we had an eternity to absorb the wisdom of the world. It's a call to balance living in the moment with preparing for the future through continuous learning.

2. "The purpose of life is not to be happy. It is to be useful, to be honorable, to be compassionate, to have it make some difference that you have lived and lived well." - Ralph Waldo Emerson

Emerson shifts the focus from personal happiness to the impact one's life has on others and the world. This quote suggests that a life well-lived is characterized by usefulness, honor, and compassion. It's about making a positive difference and leaving a legacy of kindness and meaningful contributions, implying that true fulfillment comes from what we give rather than what we get.

3. "In the end, it's not the years in your life that count. It's the life in your years." - Abraham Lincoln

Lincoln's words remind us that the value of life is not measured by its duration but by the depth and quality of our experiences. It's a call to live fully, with purpose and intensity, making each moment count. The quote encourages us to focus on filling our lives with meaningful activities, relationships, and achievements, rather than simply accumulating years.

Abraham Lincoln was an American lawyer, politician, and statesman who served as the 16th president of the United States from 1861 until his assassination in 1865.

Born: February 12, 1809, Larue County, KY
Assassinated: April 15, 1865

4. "Do not go where the path may lead, go instead where there is no path and leave a trail." - Ralph Waldo Emerson

This quote inspires individuality and pioneering spirit. Emerson encourages us to forge our own paths in life rather than following the well-trodden routes of others. It's about innovation, bravery, and leadership, creating a legacy that others might follow. The essence of the quote is to live boldly and authentically, making unique contributions to the world.

5. "Only a life lived for others is a life worthwhile." - Albert Einstein

Einstein emphasizes the importance of altruism and service to others. This quote suggests that true fulfillment and purpose are found not in self-centered pursuits but in dedicating oneself to the well-being of others. It promotes the idea that the most meaningful lives are those that contribute positively to the lives of the people around us.

6. "To live is the rarest thing in the world. Most people exist, that is all." - Oscar Wilde

Wilde's quote criticizes complacency and mere existence without purpose or passion. It distinguishes between merely existing and truly living—a life filled with passion, purpose, and active engagement with the world. Wilde encourages us to seek depth, meaning, and authenticity in our lives.

7. "Life is what happens when you're busy making other plans." - John Lennon

Lennon's quote highlights the unpredictable nature of life and the importance of being open to the unexpected. It reminds us to be present and appreciate life as it unfolds, rather than being overly focused on future plans. The quote encourages flexibility and finding joy in the journey, not just the destination.

John Winston Ono Lennon was an English singer, songwriter and musician who gained worldwide fame as the founder, co-songwriter, co-lead vocalist and rhythm guitarist of the Beatles. His work included music, writing, drawings, and film.

Born: October 9, 1940, Liverpool Maternity Hospital
Assassinated: December 8, 1980

8. "I am not what happened to me, I am what I choose to become." - Carl Jung

Jung's quote speaks to personal agency and the power of choice in defining our lives. Despite the challenges and events that befall us, this quote reminds us that we have the capacity to shape our destiny through our responses and decisions. It champions resilience, growth, and self-determination.

9. "Life is either a daring adventure or nothing at all." - Helen Keller

Keller, despite her own physical limitations, lived a life of remarkable achievement and advocacy. This quote inspires us to embrace life's challenges and opportunities with courage and zeal. It suggests that a fulfilling life is built on the willingness to take risks and explore the unknown.

10. "Not how long, but how well you have lived is the main thing."   - Seneca

The Stoic philosopher Seneca emphasizes the quality of life over its quantity. This quote is a reminder that living well involves making wise choices, cultivating virtues, and cherishing relationships. It's about the legacy we leave and the impact we have, rather than merely the span of our years.

Lucius Annaeus Seneca the Younger, usually known as Seneca, was a Stoic philosopher of Ancient Rome, a statesman, dramatist, and in one work, satirist, from the post-Augustan age of Latin literature.
Born: Córdoba, Spain
Died: 65 AD, Rome, Italy

Chapter 7. Love quotes

These quotes about love explore its multifaceted nature, from the importance of mutual growth and shared visions to the value of appreciation and selflessness. Love, as depicted through these lenses, is both a source of profound happiness and a journey of continuous learning and mutual respect.

1."We accept the love we think we deserve." - Stephen Chbosky, The Perks of Being a Wallflower

This quote suggests that our self-esteem and self-worth influence the kinds of relationships we allow ourselves to engage in. It highlights the importance of recognizing our own value to ensure we do not settle for relationships that do not fully honor or respect us.

2. "Love does not consist in gazing at each other, but in looking outward together in the same direction." - Antoine de Saint-Exupéry

Saint-Exupéry points out that true love goes beyond the initial attraction and mutual admiration. It's about sharing common goals, dreams, and values, and working together towards a shared future. This perspective emphasizes the partnership aspect of love, highlighting that a deep connection is built on more than just physical or emotional attraction.

3. "The best love is the kind that awakens the soul and makes us reach for more, that plants a fire in our hearts and brings peace to our minds." - Nicholas Sparks, The Notebook

Sparks describes a transformative kind of love that not only ignites passion but also brings a sense of peace and fulfillment. This quote speaks to the power of love to inspire growth and bring out the best in us, suggesting that the most profound relationships are those that challenge and support us in equal measure.

Nicholas Charles Sparks is an American romance novelist, screenwriter, and film producer. He has published twenty-three novels, all New York Times bestsellers, and two works of non-fiction, with over 115 million copies sold worldwide in more than 50 languages.

Born: 1965 , Omaha, NE

4. "To love and be loved is to feel the sun from both sides." - David Viscott

Viscott likens the experience of mutual love to feeling the warmth of the sun from all directions. It's a metaphor for the enveloping, all-encompassing nature of love that is both given and received, highlighting the complete sense of joy and fulfillment that comes from a reciprocal loving relationship.

5. "Love is not about possession. Love is about appreciation."   - Osho

Osho challenges the often-possessive nature of romantic love, suggesting that true love is about appreciating the other person for who they are, without trying to own or control them. This quote encourages a selfless, giving approach to love that values the happiness and freedom of the loved one.

6. "Love is that condition in which the happiness of another person is essential to your own." - Robert A. Heinlein

Heinlein defines love as a deep empathy and connection where one's happiness is intrinsically linked to the happiness of their partner. This quote captures the altruistic nature of love, where the well-being of the loved one becomes a critical component of one's own joy.

7. "The greatest happiness you can have is knowing that you do not necessarily require happiness." - William Saroyan

While not explicitly about love, this quote by Saroyan can apply to relationships by suggesting that true contentment comes from within, not from external sources or even from the relationship itself. It is a reminder that self-sufficiency and inner peace are foundational to a healthy, happy love life.

William Saroyan was an Armenian-American novelist, playwright, and short story writer. He was awarded the Pulitzer Prize for Drama in 1940, and in 1943 won the Academy Award for Best Story for the film The Human Comedy.

Born: August 31, 1908, Fresno, CA
Died: May 18, 1981

Chapter 8. Friendship quotes

Each of these quotes' sheds light on different facets of friendship, from the joy and solidarity it brings to our lives to the importance of loyalty, understanding, and mutual connection. True friendship is depicted as a treasure that enriches the human experience, providing support, laughter, and a sense of belonging.

1."Friendship is born at that moment when one person says to another, 'What! You too? I thought I was the only one.'" - C.S. Lewi

Lewis highlights a foundational moment in the birth of a friendship: the realization of shared experiences or feelings. This quote speaks to the instant connection felt when we discover common ground with someone else, emphasizing that friendship often starts with understanding and mutual recognition.

2. "A real friend is one who walks in when the rest of the world walks out." - Walter Winchell

Winchell's words underscore the loyalty and steadfastness of true friendship. In times of crisis or when we face challenges, a true friend shows their worth by staying by our side, offering support and companionship when we need it most, unlike fair-weather friends who may disappear.

3. "The only way to have a friend is to be one." - Ralph Waldo Emerson

Emerson conveys the active nature of friendship, suggesting that to experience the joys of friendship, one must also embody the qualities of a good friend. This includes being supportive, understanding, and present for others, emphasizing that friendship is a two-way street.

Ralph Waldo Emerson, who went by his middle name Waldo, was an American essayist, lecturer, philosopher, abolitionist, and poet who led the Transcendentalist movement of the mid-19th century.

Born: May 25, 1803, Boston, MA
Died: April 27, 1882

4. "In the sweetness of friendship let there be laughter and sharing of pleasures. For in the dew of little things the heart finds its morning and is refreshed." - Khalil Gibran

Gibran celebrates the joy and rejuvenation that friendship brings into our lives. He highlights the importance of sharing both laughter and simple pleasures, suggesting that these moments are what refresh and renew us, much like morning dew refreshes the earth.

5. "Friendship is not about who you have known the longest... It's about who walked into your life, said 'I'm here for you,' and proved it." – Unknown

This quote shifts the focus from the duration of a friendship to the quality and depth of the connection. It emphasizes actions over time, valuing friends who demonstrate their loyalty and support in tangible ways.

6. "Good friends are like stars. You don't always see them, but you know they're always there." – Unknown

This metaphorical quote compares true friends to stars, invisible during the day but ever-present and reliable. It speaks to the enduring nature of friendship, even when friends are not constantly visible or actively communicating, their support and love are constant and dependable.

7. "Friendship multiplies the good of life and divides its evils." - Baltasar Gracián

Gracián captures the essence of friendship as a force that amplifies joy and mitigates suffering. Friends enhance the positive experiences in life and provide support that lessens the impact of negative ones, showcasing the profound effect friendship has on our overall well-being.

Baltasar Gracián y Morales, S.J., better known as Baltasar Gracián, was a Spanish Jesuit and Baroque prose writer and philosopher. He was born in Belmonte, near Calatayud. His writings were lauded by Schopenhauer and Nietzsche.

Born: January 8, 1601, Belmonte de Gracián, Spain
Died: December 6, 1658

8. "It is not a lack of love, but a lack of friendship that makes unhappy marriages." - Friedrich Nietzsche

Nietzsche suggests that the foundation of a strong and happy marriage is friendship. This quote implies that love alone might not sustain a relationship over time without the companionship, mutual understanding, and shared joy that friendship brings.

9. "One loyal friend is worth ten thousand relatives." – Euripides

The ancient playwright Euripides highlights the immense value of a loyal friend, suggesting that the depth and quality of such a relationship can surpass even familial ties. This quote speaks to the irreplaceable role a true friend can play in one's life.

10. "Friends are the family we choose for ourselves." - Edna Buchanan

Buchanan's words highlight the unique and voluntary nature of friendship. Unlike family, which is determined by birth, friendships are formed through choice, based on mutual respect, affection, and shared values. This quote celebrates the intentional aspect of creating our own circle of support.

Edna Buchanan is an American journalist and writer who is best known for her crime mystery novels. She won the 1986 Pulitzer Prize for General News Reporting "for her versatile and consistently excellent police beat reporting."

Born: 1939

Chapter 9. Happiness quotes

These quotes offer a unique perspective on happiness, from the importance of perspective and gratitude to the role of personal agency and integrity. Together, they paint a picture of happiness as a complex, multifaceted experience that is both a journey and a choice, deeply intertwined with how we live our lives and interact with the world around us.

Happiness is a universal pursuit, deeply personal yet universally understood. Here are some of the best quotes about happiness, each followed by an explanation to uncover their deeper insights:

1."Happiness is not something ready-made. It comes from your own actions." - Dalai Lama

This quote suggests that happiness is not a passive state to be found but an active one to be created through our actions and choices. It emphasizes personal responsibility in cultivating happiness, highlighting that our actions and attitudes significantly influence our sense of well-being.

2. "For every minute you are angry you lose sixty seconds of happiness." - Ralph Waldo Emerson

Emerson's words remind us of the fleeting nature of life and the importance of choosing happiness over anger. This quote encourages us to let go of negative emotions that can consume our time and detract from our ability to experience joy.

3. "The happiest people don't have the best of everything, they just make the best of everything." – Unknown

This quote highlights that happiness is more about perspective than material circumstances. It suggests that finding joy in life does not depend on having the best of everything but in appreciating and making the most of what we have.

The 14th Dalai Lama, known to the Tibetan people as Gyalwa Rinpoche, is, as the incumbent Dalai Lama, the highest spiritual leader and head of Tibet

Born: July 6, 1935

4. "Happiness is when what you think, what you say, and what you do are in harmony." - Mahatma Gandhi

Gandhi points to the congruence of thoughts, words, and actions as the foundation of happiness. This quote emphasizes the importance of integrity and authenticity, suggesting that true happiness arises from living in a way that is consistent with our values and beliefs.

5. "The purpose of our lives is to be happy." - Dalai Lama

By stating that the purpose of life is happiness, the Dalai Lama simplifies the complex pursuits of human existence into a single, attainable goal. This perspective encourages us to prioritize joy and well-being in our daily lives and in our broader life choices.

6. "Happiness is not the absence of problems, but the ability to deal with them." – Unknown

This quote acknowledges that life will inevitably include challenges, but happiness comes from our resilience and ability to navigate difficulties. It suggests that happiness is less about a perfect life and more about the strength and attitude we bring to the problems we face.

7. "It is not how much we have, but how much we enjoy, that makes happiness." - Charles Spurgeon

Spurgeon's words highlight the importance of appreciation and contentment in finding happiness. This quote suggests that the measure of our happiness is not in the quantity of our possessions but in our capacity to find joy in what we have.

8. "Happiness cannot be traveled to, owned, earned, worn or consumed. Happiness is the spiritual experience of living every minute with love, grace, and gratitude." - Denis Waitley

Waitley describes happiness as a state of being that transcends material pursuits, emphasizing it as a spiritual experience marked by love, grace, and gratitude. This quote encourages us to cultivate happiness through our approach to life and our interactions with others.

9. "The only joy in the world is to begin." - Cesare Pavese

Pavese speaks to the excitement and happiness that come from embarking on new journeys or projects. This quote suggests that taking the first steps in any endeavor is a significant source of joy, highlighting the value of initiative and the thrill of beginnings.

10. "Happiness is not a station you arrive at, but a manner of traveling." - Margaret Lee Runbeck

Runbeck likens happiness to the journey itself, rather than a destination to be reached. This metaphor encourages us to find joy in the process and the present moment, rather than placing our happiness in future achievements or milestones.

Margaret Lee Runbeck was an **American author, educator, and social activist** known for her thought-provoking novels and insightful essays. Born on June 30, 1905, in Minnesota, Runbeck grew up in a household that valued education, creativity, and social justice.

Born: 1905
Died: 1956

Chapter 10. Wisdom quotes

These quotes collectively highlight that wisdom is more than accumulated knowledge, it's the application of that knowledge in practical, insightful ways. Wisdom involves humility, the ability to learn from experiences (including mistakes), and the capacity to find depth and meaning in the fabric of everyday life.

Wisdom is often seen as the culmination of knowledge, experience, and deep understanding, offering insights into life's complexities. Here are some of the best quotes about wisdom, each followed by an explanation to highlight their meanings:

1."The only true wisdom is in knowing you know nothing."
– Socrates

Socrates emphasizes the importance of intellectual humility in the pursuit of wisdom. Recognizing our own ignorance is the first step toward learning and gaining true wisdom. This quote suggests that wisdom comes from an ongoing quest for knowledge and an openness to new insights.

2. "Wisdom is not a product of schooling but of the lifelong attempt to acquire it." - Albert Einstein

Einstein differentiates between formal education and the broader, continuous pursuit of knowledge that defines wisdom. This quote underlines that wisdom is accumulated over a lifetime through experiences, reflections, and an unending desire to understand the world more deeply.

3. "The invariable mark of wisdom is to see the miraculous in the common." - Ralph Waldo Emerson

Emerson points out that wisdom allows individuals to appreciate the extraordinary in everyday life. This quote speaks to the ability of the wise to find beauty, wonder, and lessons in ordinary experiences and moments, suggesting that wisdom enriches life by deepening our appreciation of the world around us.

Socrates was a Greek philosopher from Athens who is credited as the founder of Western philosophy and among the first moral philosophers of the ethical tradition of thought.

Born: Alopece
Died: February 15, 399 BC

4. "Wisdom is the reward for a lifetime of listening when you'd have preferred to talk." - Doug Larson

Larson humorously yet insightfully highlights listening as a key path to wisdom. The quote suggests that by listening more than we speak, we open ourselves up to learning from others, gaining insights, and understanding different perspectives, which collectively contribute to wisdom.

5. "It is the province of knowledge to speak, and it is the privilege of wisdom to listen." - Oliver Wendell Holmes Sr.

Similar to Larson's perspective, Holmes distinguishes between knowledge and wisdom, elevating wisdom as the ability to listen and absorb. This quote emphasizes that while knowledge enables us to share and communicate, wisdom bestows the discernment to listen and learn from the world around us.

6. "Wisdom comes from experience. Experience is often a result of lack of wisdom." - Terry Pratchett

Pratchett offers a witty take on the cyclical relationship between wisdom and experience. This quote humorously suggests that our mistakes and the experiences they lead to are valuable sources of wisdom, highlighting the growth and learning that come from our less wise decisions.

7. "Knowledge is knowing a tomato is a fruit; wisdom is not putting it in a fruit salad." - Miles Kington

Kington uses humor to differentiate between knowledge and wisdom. Knowing facts, such as a tomato's classification as a fruit, represents knowledge. Wisdom, however, is the practical application of that knowledge, such as understanding that despite being a fruit, a tomato may not suit a fruit salad.

8. "Wisdom is the power to put our time and our knowledge to the proper use." - Thomas J. Watson

Watson sees wisdom as the judicious use of our resources, namely time and knowledge. This quote underscores that wisdom involves not just acquiring knowledge but also understanding how to apply it effectively and make the most of our time.

9. "He who learns must suffer. And even in our sleep, pain that cannot forget falls drop by drop upon the heart, and in our own despair, against our will, comes wisdom to us by the awful grace of God." – Aeschylus

Aeschylus speaks to the often-painful process of gaining wisdom. This quote suggests that wisdom frequently comes through suffering and challenges, marking it as a hard-earned but invaluable asset that shapes our understanding and compassion.

10. "Do not seek to follow in the footsteps of the wise. Seek what they sought." - Matsuo Basho

Basho encourages us to pursue the essence of what drives the pursuit of wisdom rather than merely imitating the actions of those we consider wise. This quote invites us to understand the underlying principles and questions that guide the wise, thus embarking on our own unique journey toward wisdom.

Matsuo Bashō , later known as Matsuo Chūemon Munefusa was the most famous poet of the Edo period in Japan. During his lifetime, Bashō was recognized for his works in the collaborative haikai no renga form; today, after centuries of commentary, he is recognized as the greatest master of haiku.

Born: 1644, Ahai district

Died: November 28, 1694

Nelson Rolihlahla Mandela was a South African anti-apartheid activist and politician who served as the first president of South Africa from 1994 to 1999. He was the country's first black head of state and the first elected in a fully representative democratic election.

Born: July 18, 1918, Mvezo, South Africa
Died: December 5, 2013

Chapter 11. Educational quotes

These educational quotes collectively underscore the multifaceted value of education in fostering intellectual and personal growth, nurturing critical thinking and character, and empowering individuals to make meaningful contributions to society. Through these lenses, education is revealed not just as a path to knowledge, but as a journey of lifelong learning and transformation.

Education is a powerful tool that shapes minds, transforms societies, and opens doors to new worlds. Here are some of the best educational quotes, each followed by an explanation to illuminate their deeper significance:

1."Education is the most powerful weapon which you can use to change the world." - Nelson Mandela

Mandela recognized education as a transformative force capable of reshaping societies and fostering global change. This quote emphasizes that through education, individuals gain the knowledge, skills, and critical thinking necessary to challenge injustices and contribute to societal progress.

2. "The function of education is to teach one to think intensively and to think critically. Intelligence plus character – that is the goal of true education." - Martin Luther King Jr.

King highlights the dual purpose of education: to cultivate both intellect and character. This quote suggests that true education goes beyond mere academic achievement; it involves nurturing ethical, compassionate individuals who can make wise decisions and contribute positively to society.

3. "Live as if you were to die tomorrow. Learn as if you were to live forever." - Mahatma Gandhi

Gandhi's words encourage a lifelong pursuit of learning, emphasizing the value of curiosity and continuous self-improvement. This quote inspires an attitude of perpetual openness to new knowledge and experiences, suggesting that education is not confined to youth or formal settings but is a lifelong journey.

4. "Education is not preparation for life; education is life itself." - John Dewey

Dewey challenges the notion that education is merely a means to an end, arguing instead that it is a vital part of life itself. This quote implies that the process of learning and growing through education is integral to human experience, enriching our understanding of the world and our place within it.

5. "It is the mark of an educated mind to be able to entertain a thought without accepting it." – Aristotle

Aristotle speaks to the importance of critical thinking, a cornerstone of education. This quote suggests that an educated individual possesses the ability to consider different viewpoints and ideas critically, without necessarily adopting them as their own. It underscores the value of open-mindedness and the capacity for independent judgment.

6. "Education is the passport to the future, for tomorrow belongs to those who prepare for it today." - Malcolm X

Malcolm X underscores the forward-looking nature of education, viewing it as essential preparation for future success. This quote highlights that by investing in education today, individuals can secure a brighter, more prosperous future for themselves and their communities.

7. "The beautiful thing about learning is that no one can take it away from you." - B.B. King

King celebrates the enduring value of education, emphasizing that knowledge and skills, once acquired, are permanent personal assets. This quote reminds us that education empowers individuals in a way that material possessions cannot, offering a form of wealth that is immune to loss or theft.

8. "The mind is not a vessel to be filled, but a fire to be kindled." – Plutarch

Plutarch challenges the traditional view of education as the transmission of information, advocating instead for a model that inspires curiosity, creativity, and critical thinking. This quote suggests that the goal of education is to stimulate minds, encouraging students to explore, question, and discover.

9. "Change is the end result of all true learning." - Leo Buscaglia

Buscaglia connects education with transformation, suggesting that genuine learning always results in change, whether in perspective, understanding, or behavior. This quote highlights the dynamic nature of education as a catalyst for personal growth and evolution.

10. "Education is the key to unlocking the world, a passport to freedom." - Oprah Winfrey

Oprah likens education to a key and passport, metaphors that evoke its role in opening doors to opportunities and granting individuals the freedom to pursue their dreams. This quote reflects the empowering effect of education in overcoming barriers and achieving personal and professional fulfillment.

Oprah Gail Winfrey, also known as Oprah, is an American talk show host, television producer, actress, author, and media proprietor. She is best known for her talk show, The Oprah Winfrey Show, broadcast from Chicago, which ran in national syndication for 25 years, from 1986 to 2011.

Born: January 29, 1954

Chapter 12. Nature quotes

These quotes collectively underscore the profound impact nature has on our lives, offering wisdom, peace, and a sense of belonging. They remind us of the importance of preserving and cherishing the natural world, not only for its aesthetic and recreational value but also for its integral role in our physical and spiritual well-being.

Nature, with its profound beauty and complexity, has inspired countless reflections on life, existence, and our place within the world. Here are some of the best quotes about nature, each followed by an in-depth explanation to unpack their deeper meanings:

1. "In every walk with nature, one receives far more than he seeks." - John Muir

John Muir, often considered the father of national parks, believed that nature has a generous spirit. This quote suggests that by engaging with the natural world, we gain not only physical benefits but also spiritual and emotional nourishment. Nature offers insights, moments of awe, and a sense of connection that surpasses our initial intentions or expectations when we set out to explore it.

2. "The clearest way into the Universe is through a forest wilderness." - John Muir

Here, Muir articulates the idea that to truly understand the vastness and complexity of the universe, one must immerse oneself in the untouched wilderness. Forests, in their primal state, act as gateways to a deeper understanding of the world and our place within it, providing a direct connection to the essence of life and the cosmos.

3. "Look deep into nature, and then you will understand everything better." - Albert Einstein

Einstein, renowned for his contributions to physics, recognized nature as a source of revelation and wisdom. This quote highlights the idea that by observing and reflecting on natural phenomena, we can gain insights into the fundamental principles that govern the universe and, as a result, achieve a greater understanding of all aspects of life.

4. "Nature does not hurry, yet everything is accomplished." - Lao Tzu

The Taoist philosopher Lao Tzu points to the effortless efficiency of nature as a model for human action. This quote encourages patience and trust in the natural flow of events, suggesting that a harmonious and balanced approach to life, free from the rush and urgency that often characterize human endeavors, can lead to fulfillment and success.

5. "The earth has music for those who listen." - William Shakespeare

Shakespeare, in his poetic way, reminds us of the subtle beauty and rhythms of the natural world. This quote implies that nature communicates with us through its sounds, patterns, and cycles, offering beauty and inspiration to those who are attentive and receptive to its melodies.

6. "Adopt the pace of nature: her secret is patience." - Ralph Waldo Emerson

Emerson, a profound advocate of the transcendentalist movement, believed in the wisdom of aligning human life with the principles of nature. This quote specifically highlights patience as a virtue demonstrated by nature, suggesting that many of life's challenges can be navigated successfully with a patient, enduring approach.

7. "Nature is not a place to visit. It is home." - Gary Snyder

Snyder, a poet known for his environmental activism, challenges the notion of nature as separate from human existence. This quote is a poignant reminder that humans are intrinsically part of the natural world, and it calls for a deeper respect and connection to the environment, recognizing it as our essential habitat.

8. "Those who contemplate the beauty of the earth find reserves of strength that will endure as long as life lasts." - Rachel Carson

Carson, a marine biologist, and conservationist, suggests that the appreciation of nature's beauty provides not only immediate pleasure but also a lasting source of strength and resilience. This quote emphasizes the enduring impact of nature on our well-being and spirit, advocating for its preservation as a source of sustenance for the human soul.

9. "The mountains are calling, and I must go." - John Muir

This famous declaration by Muir captures the irresistible pull of nature and the deep, instinctive connection many feel towards the wilderness. It speaks to the human yearning for exploration, adventure, and communion with the natural world, suggesting that such experiences are essential to our identity and well-being.

10. "We do not see nature with our eyes, but with our understandings and our hearts." - William Hazlitt

Hazlitt, an essayist, implies that true appreciation of nature goes beyond mere visual perception. It involves an emotional and intellectual engagement that allows us to truly connect with and understand the natural world. This quote suggests that the beauty and lessons of nature are best grasped with an open heart and a thoughtful mind.

William Hazlitt was an English essayist, drama and literary critic, painter, social commentator, and philosopher. He is now considered one of the greatest critics and essayists in the history of the English language, placed in the company of Samuel Johnson and George Orwell.

Born: April 10, 1778, Maidstone, United Kingdom
Died: September 18, 1830

Chapter 13. Humorous quotes

These quotes cleverly use humor to comment on life's ironies, the human condition, and everyday observations. They remind us that laughter can offer not just amusement but also insight, providing a lighter perspective on the complexities of life.

Humor has a unique way of shedding light on life's complexities, offering relief and perspective through laughter. Here are some of the best humorous quotes, each followed by an explanation that delves into their wit and wisdom:

1."I am so clever that sometimes I don't understand a single word of what I am saying." - Oscar Wilde

Wilde, known for his sharp wit, humorously comments on the complexity of his own thoughts and the elaborate way he expresses them. This self-deprecating joke highlights the irony in being so intellectually advanced that one's ideas become incomprehensible, even to oneself. It's a playful nod to the absurdity of intellectual pretension.

2. "The difference between stupidity and genius is that genius has its limits." - Albert Einstein

Einstein's quip cleverly points out that stupidity can be boundless, whereas genius, no matter how expansive, has its limits. This humorous observation serves as a commentary on the human condition, suggesting that the capacity for foolishness can be surprisingly infinite, whereas intellectual brilliance, though vast, is not without its boundaries.

3. "Life is like a sewer... what you get out of it depends on what you put into it." - Tom Lehrer

Lehrer, a mathematician, and satirist, uses the metaphor of a sewer to comment on life's reciprocity. The humor lies in comparing life to something as unglamorous as a sewer, but the underlying message is insightful: life's outcomes often reflect our efforts and contributions. It's a wry reminder to invest wisely in our lives.

Thomas Andrew Lehrer is an American musician, singer-songwriter, satirist, and mathematician, who later taught mathematics and musical theater. He recorded pithy and humorous songs that became popular in the 1950s and 1960s. His songs often parodied popular musical forms, though they usually had original melodies.

Born: 1928

4. "I refuse to join any club that would have me as a member." - Groucho Marx

Marx's famous quip encapsulates self-deprecating humor and skepticism about social acceptance. By ironically stating he wouldn't want to be part of a club that would accept someone like him, Marx humorously comments on human insecurities and the absurdity of social elitism.

5. "A Day without laughter is a day wasted." - Charlie Chaplin

Chaplin, celebrated for his comedic genius, underscores the essential role of laughter in life. This quote, while humorous in its mandate, serves as a poignant reminder of the value of joy and humor. It suggests that laughter enriches our days and that without it, life is less fulfilling.

6. "If you try to fail, and succeed, which have you done?" - George Carlin

Carlin, known for his incisive and satirical humor, presents a paradoxical scenario that playfully explores the concepts of success and failure. This humorous riddle invites us to ponder the nature of our intentions and outcomes, highlighting the often blurry line between failing and succeeding.

7. "The road to success is dotted with many tempting parking spaces." - Will Rogers

Rogers humorously acknowledges the distractions and temptations that can sidetrack us on our journey to success. This quote uses the metaphor of a road with appealing parking spaces to comment on the discipline required to stay focused on our goals, despite the allure of comfort and procrastination.

8. "Be careful about reading health books. You may die of a misprint." - Mark Twain

Twain's wit shines through in this caution against taking health advice from books too seriously, humorously suggesting that a simple typographical error could have fatal consequences. It's a lighthearted reminder of the importance of skepticism and the potential pitfalls of relying too heavily on written authority, especially regarding health.

9. "I'm writing a book. I've got the page numbers done." - Steven Wright

Wright, known for his deadpan humor, delivers a comically literal take on the process of writing a book. This joke plays on the expectation of substantive progress by focusing instead on a trivial aspect, highlighting the humor in procrastination and minimal achievement.

10. "I haven't spoken to my wife in years. I didn't want to interrupt her." - Rodney Dangerfield

Dangerfield, famous for his self-deprecating humor and catchphrase "I don't get no respect," jokes about the dynamics of marital communication. This quote humorously exaggerates the notion of not wanting to interrupt, suggesting a long period of silence as a form of respect or perhaps a commentary on the nature of listening within relationships.

Jack Roy, better known by the pseudonym Rodney Dangerfield, was an American stand-up comedian, actor, screenwriter, and producer. He was known for his self-deprecating one-liner humor, his catchphrase "I don't get no respect!" and his monologues on that theme.

Born: November 22, 1921, Deer Park, NY
Died: October 5, 2004

Chapter 14. Philosophical quotes

These philosophical quotes open doors to deep contemplation, challenging us to question and reflect on our beliefs, existence, and the nature of reality. They serve as gateways to the vast landscapes of philosophical inquiry, inviting us to explore the depths of human thought and understanding.

Philosophical quotes delve deep into the essence of existence, knowledge, ethics, and the universe, challenging our perceptions and encouraging profound reflection. Here are some of the best philosophical quotes, each accompanied by an explanation to illuminate their meanings:

1. "The unexamined life is not worth living." - Socrates

Socrates emphasizes the importance of self-reflection and critical thinking. By stating that an unexamined life is not worth living, he suggests that the essence of life is found in questioning and understanding oneself and the world around us. It's a call to pursue wisdom and moral inquiry as fundamental to a life of value and meaning.

2. "One cannot step into the same river twice." – Heraclitus

Heraclitus highlights the constant flux and change in the universe. This quote metaphorically suggests that everything is in a state of continuous transformation, including ourselves and our experiences. It challenges the notion of permanence and encourages acceptance of change as a fundamental aspect of existence.

3. "Man is condemned to be free; because once thrown into the world, he is responsible for everything he does." - Jean-Paul Sartre

Sartre, a leading existentialist, addresses the burden of freedom. He suggests that with the absence of predetermined essence or purpose, humans are entirely free to make their choices but are also wholly responsible for the consequences. This quote underscores the weight of freedom and the inherent responsibility of creating one's essence through actions.

Jean-Paul Charles Aymard Sartre was a French philosopher, playwright, novelist, screenwriter, political activist, biographer, and literary critic, considered a leading figure in 20th-century French philosophy and Marxism. Sartre was one of the key figures in the philosophy of existentialism.

Born: June 21, 1905, Paris, France
Died: April 15, 1980

4. "The only thing I know is that I know nothing." – Socrates

This statement, known as the Socratic Paradox, captures Socrates' approach to wisdom. By acknowledging his own ignorance, Socrates points to the vastness of knowledge yet to be discovered and the importance of maintaining an open, questioning attitude. It's a profound admission of humility and the starting point for genuine inquiry and learning.

5. "God is dead! He remains dead! And we have killed him!" - Friedrich Nietzsche

Nietzsche's provocative declaration in "The Gay Science" is often misunderstood. He is not celebrating the death of the deity but rather commenting on the declining power of traditional Christian morality and belief in the modern world. This quote challenges us to confront the implications of a world where traditional moral anchors no longer hold sway, questioning how values and meaning can be constructed in the absence of divine authority.

6. "The master has failed more times than the beginner has even tried." - Stephen McCranie

This quote, while simpler than others in this list, conveys an essential truth about mastery and learning. McCranie underscores that failure is a crucial part of the learning process and that perseverance in the face of failure is what distinguishes the master from the novice. It's a philosophical reflection on the nature of learning, growth, and resilience.

7. "If God did not exist, it would be necessary to invent Him." – Voltaire

Voltaire's statement is a commentary on the societal and moral function of religion. He suggests that even if God were a human invention, the concept serves essential purposes, such as providing moral guidance and comfort in the face of existential questions. It's a reflection on the human need for belief systems to make sense of life's complexities.

François-Marie Arouet, known by his nom de plume M. de Voltaire, was a French Enlightenment writer, philosopher, satirist, and historian. Famous for his wit and his criticism of Christianity and of slavery, Voltaire was an advocate of freedom of speech, freedom of religion, and separation of church and state.
Born: November 21, 1694, Paris, France
Died: May 30, 1778

8. "Liberty consists in doing what one desires." - John Stuart Mill

Mill, a philosopher and economist, defines liberty in terms of the ability to pursue one's desires, assuming these do not harm others. This quote is foundational to liberal political philosophy, emphasizing individual freedom as essential to happiness and social progress. It challenges us to consider the balance between personal freedom and social responsibility.

9. "To be is to be perceived." - George Berkeley

Berkeley, an idealist philosopher, posits that existence is dependent on perception. His assertion challenges materialist conceptions of reality, suggesting that objects only exist to the extent that they are perceived by a consciousness. It's a radical inquiry into the nature of existence and the relationship between mind and matter.

10. "I think, therefore I am." - René Descartes

Descartes' cogito argument is a cornerstone of Western philosophy. In doubting everything that can possibly be doubted, Descartes arrives at the undeniable truth of his own existence as a thinking entity. This quote lays the foundation for a philosophy based on the primacy of reason and individual consciousness, asserting that the act of thinking itself is proof of existence.

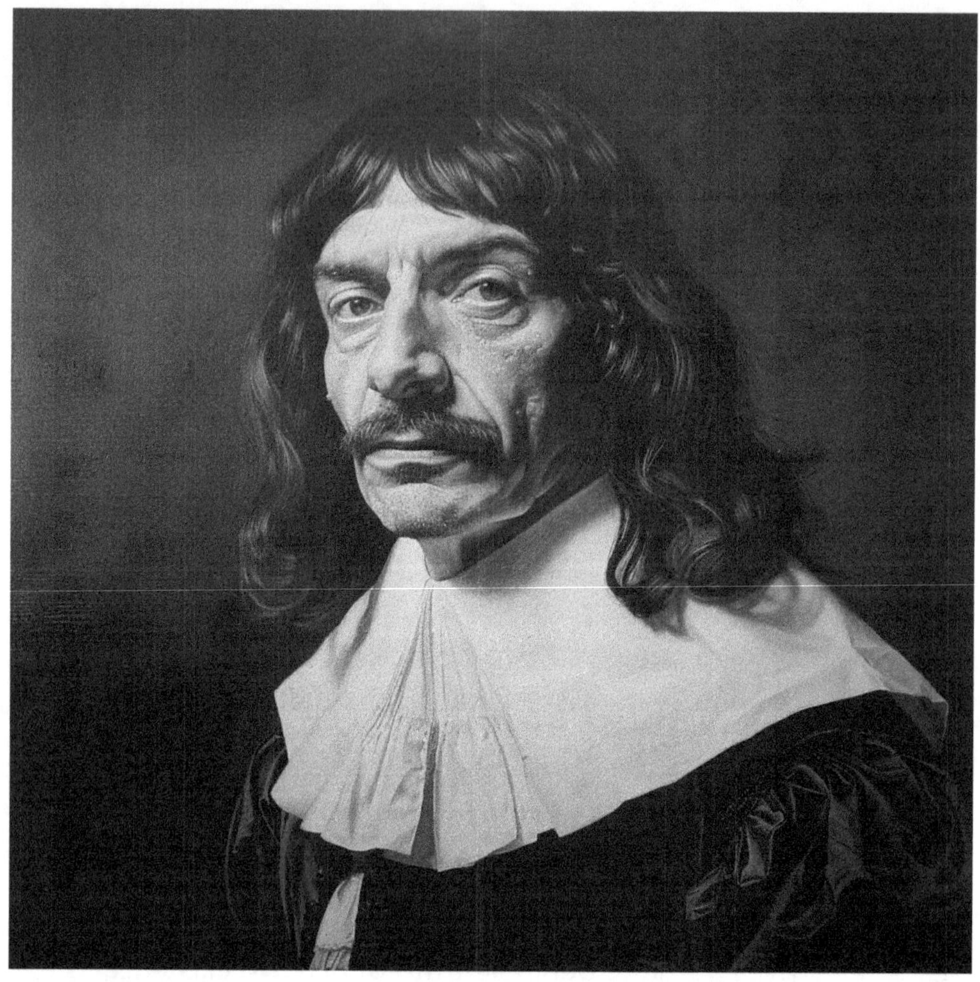

René Descartes was a French philosopher, scientist, and mathematician, widely considered a seminal figure in the emergence of modern philosophy and science. Mathematics was central to his method of inquiry, and he connected the previously separate fields of geometry and algebra into analytic geometry.

Born: March 31, 1596, Descartes, France
Died: February 11, 1650

Chapter 15. Art and creativity quotes

These quotes collectively highlight the profound impact of art and creativity on personal expression, perception, and human experience. They remind us that art is not just about aesthetic appreciation but also about communication, transformation, and a deeper engagement with life itself.

Art and creativity are vital expressions of human experience, reflecting our deepest emotions, thoughts, and visions. Here are some of the best quotes about art and creativity, each followed by an in-depth explanation to explore their profound meanings:

1."Art is not what you see, but what you make others see." - Edgar Degas

Degas highlights the transformative power of art, emphasizing its role in altering perception and evoking insight. This quote suggests that the essence of art lies in its ability to communicate and reveal new perspectives to the viewer, transcending mere visual appearance to convey deeper meaning and emotion.

2. "Creativity takes courage." - Henri Matisse

Matisse acknowledges the vulnerability involved in the creative process. This quote reflects the idea that expressing oneself artistically requires bravery, as it often involves exposing personal thoughts and feelings to public scrutiny. It's a reminder that the act of creating is inherently risky but also rewarding.

3. "The aim of art is to represent not the outward appearance of things, but their inward significance." – Aristotle

Aristotle delves into the purpose of art, suggesting it's to capture and communicate the essence or deeper truth of its subject. This quote implies that true art goes beyond mere replication of the physical world, seeking instead to reveal its underlying realities and the human condition.

Aristotle was an Ancient Greek philosopher and polymath. His writings cover a broad range of subjects spanning the natural sciences, philosophy, linguistics, economics, politics, psychology, and the arts.

Born: 384 BC, Stagira, Greece
Died: 323 BC

4. "Every child is an artist. The problem is how to remain an artist once we grow up." - Pablo Picasso

Picasso speaks to the innate creativity found in children, lamenting the tendency to lose this natural inclination as adults. This quote underscores the challenge of maintaining creativity amidst the pressures and conventions of adult life, emphasizing the importance of preserving the imaginative freedom and curiosity characteristic of childhood.

5. "Art enables us to find ourselves and lose ourselves at the same time." - Thomas Merton

Merton captures the paradoxical nature of art as both a means of self-discovery and a form of escapism. This quote reflects on art's capacity to connect us with our deepest selves while also providing a sanctuary from the external world, highlighting its role in personal and spiritual exploration.

6. "I dream my painting and I paint my dream." - Vincent van Gogh

Van Gogh's words reveal the deeply personal and visionary aspect of creating art. This quote suggests that the act of painting (or any creative endeavor) is a way to bring one's inner visions and dreams to life, emphasizing the intimate connection between imagination and artistic expression.

7. "Art is the lie that enables us to realize the truth." - Pablo Picasso

Picasso contemplates the illusory nature of art and its capacity to convey deeper truths. This quote suggests that while art may not always represent reality accurately, it possesses the unique ability to reveal essential truths about life, humanity, and the universe, offering insights in a way that direct representation cannot.

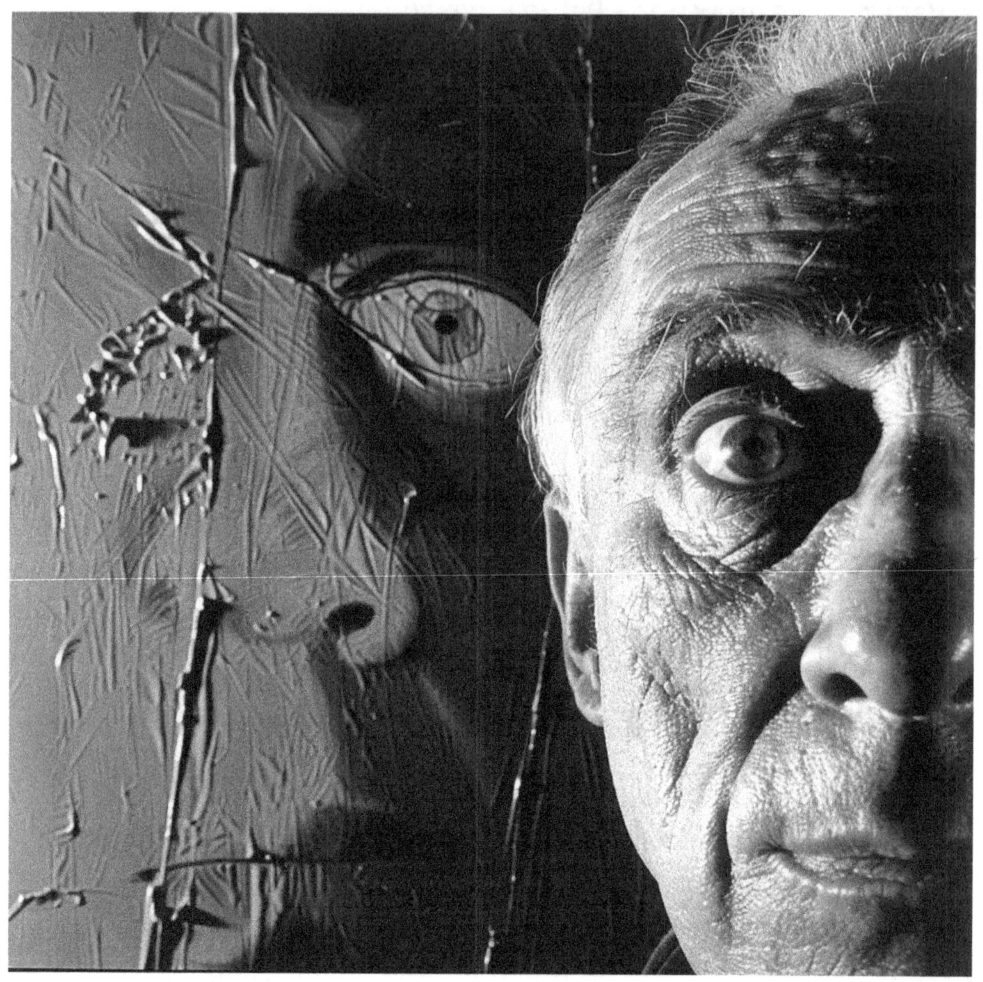

Pablo Ruiz Picasso was a Spanish painter, sculptor, printmaker, ceramicist, and theatre designer who spent most of his adult life in France.

Born: October 25, 1881, Málaga, Spain
Died: April 8, 1973

8. "To be creative means to be in love with life. You can be creative only if you love life enough that you want to enhance its beauty, you want to bring a little more music to it, a little more poetry to it, a little more dance to it." – Osho

Osho links creativity directly with a love for life, suggesting that creative expression is a way of contributing beauty and vibrancy to the world. This quote highlights creativity as an act of appreciation and enhancement of life, driven by a desire to enrich the human experience through art.

9. "Art washes away from the soul the dust of everyday life." - Pablo Picasso

Picasso metaphorically describes art's cleansing effect on the human spirit. This quote suggests that engagement with art—whether as creator or observer—provides a respite from the mundanity and burdens of daily life, refreshing the soul and offering a sense of renewal.

10. "Creativity is allowing yourself to make mistakes. Art is knowing which ones to keep." - Scott Adams

Adams differentiates between the freedom of the creative process and the discernment involved in creating art. This quote acknowledges that making mistakes is an integral part of creativity, while the art lies in recognizing which of those mistakes contribute to the work's value and meaning.

Scott Raymond Adams is an American author and cartoonist. He is the creator of the Dilbert comic strip, and the author of several nonfiction works of business, commentary, and satire. Adams worked in various clerical roles before he became a full-time cartoonist in 1995.

Born: 1957

Chapter 16. Courage and Bravery Quotes

Courage and bravery are pivotal virtues that inspire us to face challenges, take risks, and stand up for our beliefs despite fear and adversity.

These quotes remind us that fear is a natural part of the human condition but facing it with fortitude allows us to live lives defined by growth, integrity, and profound strength. They inspire us to embrace vulnerability, take risks, and stand firm in our convictions, recognizing that the essence.

Here are some of the best quotes on courage and bravery, each accompanied by a thoughtful explanation to delve into their profound meanings:

1."Courage is not the absence of fear, but the triumph over it." - Nelson Mandela

Mandela teaches us that courage doesn't mean you aren't afraid; rather, it means you confront and overcome your fears. True bravery involves facing what terrifies us, acknowledging our fears, and deciding to take action despite them. It's a reminder that the essence of courage lies in the struggle against fear, not in fearlessness.

2. "The only thing we have to fear is fear itself." - Franklin D. Roosevelt

In his inaugural speech, Roosevelt addressed a nation crippled by the Great Depression, emphasizing that fear can paralyze the needed effort to convert retreat into advance. This quote underscores the idea that fear, more than any external situation, is the greatest enemy to progress and action. It's a call to face challenges with a mindset that refuses to be hindered by fear itself.

3. "I learned that courage was not the absence of fear, but the triumph over it. The brave man is not he who does not feel afraid, but he who conquers that fear." - Nelson Mandela

Echoing the sentiments of his other well-known quote, Mandela further clarifies that bravery isn't about a lack of fear but about battling and overcoming it. This reinforces the notion that experiencing fear is natural, but the true measure of courage is found in how we respond to fear.

4. "Bravery is being the only one who knows you're afraid." - Franklin P. Jones

Jones offers a nuanced perspective on bravery, suggesting that true bravery might be a deeply personal experience, unknown to those around us. It's the idea that you can be terrified internally but choose to present a composed and brave face to the world. This form of bravery is silent and individual, yet profoundly powerful.

5. "It is not the strength of the body that counts, but the strength of the spirit." - J.R.R. Tolkien

Through his literature, Tolkien emphasizes the importance of inner strength and resilience. This quote suggests that physical prowess is secondary to the strength of one's character and spirit. In many life battles, especially those involving moral choices and personal challenges, it's the courage of the heart that truly makes a difference.

6. "You cannot swim for new horizons until you have courage to lose sight of the shore." - William Faulkner

Faulkner metaphorically speaks to the necessity of leaving behind the familiar to discover new possibilities and achievements. This quote emphasizes that courage involves taking risks and stepping into the unknown, understanding that growth and discovery lie beyond the comfort of the familiar.

7. "Courage starts with showing up and letting ourselves be seen." - Brené Brown

Brené Brown, known for her research on vulnerability, highlights that courage is deeply connected to vulnerability. This quote suggests that true bravery involves the willingness to be authentic and visible in our truest form, despite the risk of judgment or failure. It's a call to embrace vulnerability as the path to genuine connection and strength.

8. "Being deeply loved gives you strength, while loving someone deeply gives you courage." - Lao Tzu

The ancient Chinese philosopher Lao Tzu reflects on the transformative power of love in granting us strength and courage. This quote implies that the experience of being loved empowers us, while the act of loving others requires courage. It highlights love as a source of profound strength and bravery.

9. "To dare is to lose one's footing momentarily. Not to dare is to lose oneself." - Søren Kierkegaard

Kierkegaard, the Danish philosopher, presents a paradox on the nature of daring and risk. This quote philosophically suggests that while taking risks may momentarily destabilize us, the failure to take risks results in a deeper loss – the loss of one's identity and potential. It champions the courage to dare as essential to self-discovery and authenticity.

10. "Courage is the first of human qualities because it is the quality which guarantees all others." - Winston Churchill

Churchill asserts the primacy of courage among human virtues. This quote proposes that courage is foundational because it enables the practice and defense of all other virtues. Without courage, values such as honesty, integrity, and compassion cannot be upheld in the face of challenges. It highlights courage as the bedrock upon which character is built.

Laozi, also Romanized as Lao Tzu and various other ways, was a semi-legendary ancient Chinese philosopher, author of the Tao Te Ching, the foundational text of Taoism along with the Zhuangzi. Laozi is a Chinese honorific, typically translated as "the Old Master".

Born: 571 BC, Chu , CHINA

Chapter 17. Mindfulness and Presence Quotes

Mindfulness and presence are key to living a balanced and fulfilling life, helping us to connect deeply with our experiences and the world around us.

These quotes underscore the importance of living with awareness, acceptance, and a deep connection to the present moment. They remind us that mindfulness is not just a practice but a way of being that enriches our experience of life, offering clarity, peace, and a profound sense of aliveness.

Here are some of the best quotes about mindfulness and presence, each followed by a detailed explanation to illuminate their deeper insights:

1."The present moment is the only time over which we have dominion." - Thich Nhat Hanh

Thich Nhat Hanh, a Zen master, emphasizes that the present moment is the only reality we can truly influence. This quote suggests that while the past is unchangeable and the future is uncertain, our power lies in the here and now. It's a call to mindfulness, encouraging us to engage fully with the present, where our actions and thoughts can have meaningful impact.

2. "Mindfulness isn't difficult, we just need to remember to do it." - Sharon Salzberg

Salzberg, a meditation teacher, addresses a common misconception about mindfulness, noting that the practice itself is straightforward—it simply requires our remembrance and commitment. This quote highlights the challenge of maintaining continuous awareness in our fast-paced, distractible lives and serves as a gentle reminder to anchor ourselves in the present.

Sharon Salzberg is an author and teacher of Buddhist meditation practices in the West. In 1974, she co-founded the Insight Meditation Society at Barre, Massachusetts, with Jack Kornfield and Joseph Goldstein.

Born: 1952 , New York, NY

**3. "Be where you are; otherwise, you will miss your life." –
Buddha**

This quote attributed to Buddha encapsulates the essence of
mindfulness—being fully present in each moment. It warns against
the mental habit of living in the past or future, which can lead us to
miss out on our actual lives unfolding in the present. It's a profound
reminder to engage with the here and now, where life truly
happens.

**4. "Life is a dance. Mindfulness is witnessing that dance." -
Amit Ray**

Amit Ray metaphorically describes life as a dance and
mindfulness as the act of observing that dance. This quote suggests
that mindfulness allows us to step back and become aware
observers of our own lives, appreciating the beauty and complexity
of our experiences without getting lost in them.

**5."Do not dwell in the past, do not dream of the future,
concentrate the mind on the present moment." – Buddha**

Another profound insight attributed to Buddha; this quote
urges us to focus our minds on the present. It highlights the futility
of clinging to the past or speculating about the future, advocating
instead for a concentrated effort to live fully in the moment, where
true life occurs and where we have the power to act and choose.

**6. "The best way to capture moments is to pay attention.
This is how we cultivate mindfulness." - Jon Kabat-Zinn**

Jon Kabat-Zinn, a pioneer in mindfulness meditation,
suggests that paying attention is the key to capturing the essence
of each moment. This quote speaks to the practice of mindfulness
as an active process of engagement with the present, where
heightened awareness enables us to experience life more fully and
deeply.

7. "Feelings come and go like clouds in a windy sky. Conscious breathing is my anchor." - Thich Nhat Hanh

Thich Nhat Hanh offers a vivid metaphor for the transient nature of emotions and the stabilizing power of mindful breathing. This quote reminds us of those feelings, no matter how intense, are temporary, and that we can find solidity and calm in the practice of focused, conscious breathing.

Thích Nhất Hạnh was a Vietnamese Thiền Buddhist monk, peace activist, prolific author, poet and teacher, who founded the Plum Village Tradition, historically recognized as the main inspiration for engaged Buddhism. Known as the "father of mindfulness", Nhất Hạnh was a major influence on Western practices of Buddhism.

Born: October 11, 1926, Hue, Vietnam

Died: January 22, 2022

8. "Mindfulness means being awake. It means knowing what you are doing." - Jon Kabat-Zinn

Here, Kabat-Zinn defines mindfulness as a state of mindfulness and conscious awareness. It's about being cognizant of our actions, thoughts, and feelings in real-time, enabling us to live intentionally rather than reactively. This quote underscores mindfulness as the foundation for deliberate living and genuine presence.

9. "Mindfulness is the aware, balanced acceptance of the present experience. It isn't more complicated than that. It is opening to or receiving the present moment, pleasant or unpleasant, just as it is, without either clinging to it or rejecting it." - Sylvia Boorstein

Boorstein provides a comprehensive definition of mindfulness, emphasizing acceptance and balance. This quote illuminate's mindfulness as the practice of fully embracing the present moment without judgment or desire to change it, fostering a state of peace and equanimity.

10. "Wherever you are, be all there." - Jim Elliot

Missionary Jim Elliot encapsulates the essence of presence in this simple yet profound statement. It's an exhortation to fully engage with the present task or situation, setting aside distractions and preoccupations to immerse oneself completely in the moment at hand.

Philip James Elliot was an American Christian missionary and one of five people killed during Operation Auca, an attempt to evangelize the Huaorani people of Ecuador.

Born: October 8, 1927, Portland, OR

Died: January 8, 1956

Chapter 18. Gratitude and appreciation Quotes

Gratitude and appreciation are powerful emotions that can transform our perspective, enhancing our well-being and fostering positive relationships.

These quotes on gratitude and appreciation illuminate the profound impact these attitudes can have on our perspective, relationships, and overall quality of life. They remind us that by fostering an orientation towards thankfulness, we can cultivate a richer, more fulfilling experience of the world.

Here are some of the best quotes on gratitude and appreciation, each followed by a detailed explanation to explore their depth and significance:

1."Gratitude makes sense of our past, brings peace for today, and creates a vision for tomorrow." - Melody Beattie

Beattie encapsulates the transformative power of gratitude in this quote. Gratitude helps us reinterpret our past experiences with a sense of thankfulness, which can bring peace and contentment in the present. Furthermore, it encourages a positive outlook towards the future, suggesting that gratitude is not just a fleeting feeling but a foundational attitude that shapes our entire life's perspective.

2. "The more you praise and celebrate your life, the more there is in life to celebrate." - Oprah Winfrey

Oprah highlights a virtuous cycle where appreciation for life amplifies the experiences and joys available to be celebrated. This quote suggests that by actively recognizing and valuing the good in our lives, we attract more positivity and reasons for joy, thereby enriching our life experience.

3. "Let us be grateful to the people who make us happy; they are the charming gardeners who make our souls blossom." - Marcel Proust

Proust acknowledges the significant impact of those who contribute to our happiness, likening them to gardeners who nurture our soul's growth and flowering. This quote emphasizes the importance of expressing gratitude towards the individuals who bring joy and fulfillment into our lives, recognizing their role in our personal development and well-being.

Valentin Louis Georges Eugène Marcel Proust was a French novelist, literary critic, and essayist who wrote the monumental novel À la recherche du temps perdu which was published in seven volumes between 1913 and 1927.

Born: July 10, 1871, Neuilly-Auteuil-Passy, France

Died: November 18, 1922

4. "Appreciation is a wonderful thing: It makes what is excellent in others belong to us as well." – Voltaire

Voltaire points out the unifying power of appreciation, suggesting that by valuing the qualities and achievements of others, we also enrich ourselves. This quote speaks to the idea that appreciation allows us to share in the excellence around us, expanding our own experiences and sense of connection.

5. "Gratitude turns what we have into enough." – Anonymous

This quote succinctly captures the essence of gratitude as a perspective that fosters contentment. By being thankful for what we already possess, we shift our focus from what we lack to what we have, fostering a sense of sufficiency and satisfaction with our present circumstances.

6. "If the only prayer you said in your whole life was, 'thank you,' that would suffice." - Meister Eckhart

Eckhart, a mystic, emphasizes the profound significance of gratitude in this quote. Suggesting that a simple expression of thanks could be the most powerful and sufficient prayer, he highlights gratitude as a fundamental acknowledgment of life's blessings, encapsulating humility, recognition, and fulfillment in two words.

7. "Gratitude is not only the greatest of virtues but the parent of all others." – Cicero

Cicero elevates gratitude to the highest virtue, proposing that it is the source from which all other virtues spring. This quote suggests that gratitude lays the foundation for other positive qualities, such as generosity, kindness, and patience, by fostering an attitude of appreciation and humility.

Marcus Tullius Cicero was a Roman statesman, lawyer, scholar, philosopher, writer and Academic skeptic, who tried to uphold optimate principles during the political crises that led to the establishment of the Roman Empire. His extensive writings include treatises on rhetoric, philosophy and politics.

Born: January 3, 106 BC, Arpino, Italy

Assassinated: December 7, 43 BC

8. "Acknowledging the good that you already have in your life is the foundation for all abundance." - Eckhart Tolle

Tolle links gratitude with the concept of abundance, suggesting that recognizing and valuing our current blessings is the basis for attracting more abundance into our lives. This quote emphasizes that an attitude of gratitude can shift our perception from scarcity to abundance, opening our hearts and lives to greater possibilities.

9."We must find time to stop and thank the people who make a difference in our lives." - John F. Kennedy

Kennedy reminds us of the importance of expressing gratitude to those who impact our lives positively. This quote encourages us to take a moment to acknowledge and appreciate the contributions of others, recognizing that such gestures strengthen relationships and foster a sense of community and connection.

10. "Silent gratitude isn't very much to anyone." - Gertrude Stein

Stein highlights the importance of expressing gratitude openly rather than keeping it to ourselves. This quote suggests that gratitude gains its true value and power when shared, as unvoiced appreciation does little to convey our thankfulness to those who deserve to hear it.

John Fitzgerald Kennedy, often referred to as JFK, was an American politician who served as the 35th president of the United States from 1961 until his assassination in 1963. He was the youngest person elected president.

Born: May 29, 1917, Brookline, MA

Assassinated: November 22, 1963

Chapter 19. Adventure and exploration Quotes

Adventure and exploration stir the human spirit, encouraging us to seek new experiences, challenge our limits, and discover the world's wonders.

These quotes capture the essence of adventure and exploration as endeavors that challenge our limits, broaden our perspectives, and enrich our lives. They remind us that the spirit of discovery lies in both the external world and the internal journey of growth.

Here are some of the best quotes on adventure and exploration, each followed by an in-depth explanation to uncover their richer meanings:

1. "Adventure is not outside man; it is within." - George Eliot

Eliot suggests that the true essence of adventure comes from an internal desire and curiosity rather than external circumstances. This quote emphasizes that our perception and willingness to seek out the new and unknown are what truly define an adventure. It's a reminder that the spirit of exploration starts within us, urging us to look inward to ignite our sense of wonder and bravery.

2. "The world is a book, and those who do not travel read only one page." - Saint Augustine

Saint Augustine uses the metaphor of the world as a book to highlight the value of travel and exploration in broadening our understanding and perspective. This quote suggests that staying in one place limits our experience and knowledge, just as reading only one page of a book would provide an incomplete story. Traveling allows us to experience different cultures, ideas, and landscapes, enriching our lives with diverse chapters of human and natural beauty.

Augustine of Hippo, also known as Saint Augustine, was a theologian and philosopher of Berber origin and the bishop of Hippo Regius in Numidia, Roman North Africa.

Born: November 13, 354 AD, Thagaste, Algeria

Died: August 28, 430 AD.

3. "To travel is to discover that everyone is wrong about other countries." - Aldous Huxley

Huxley points out that travel challenges and often disproves the stereotypes and misconceptions we hold about other places and their people. This quote emphasizes the transformative power of travel in expanding our understanding and fostering a more nuanced and empathetic view of the world. It's a call to seek firsthand experiences that allow us to form our own informed opinions.

4. "Not all those who wander are lost." - J.R.R. Tolkien

Tolkien's famous line from "The Lord of the Rings" defends the value of wandering and exploring without a fixed destination. This quote celebrates the idea that exploration is a valuable pursuit, even without a clear end goal. It suggests that the act of wandering can lead to self-discovery, unexpected adventures, and profound insights, even if it doesn't follow a conventional path.

5. "Only those who risk going too far can possibly find out how far one can go." - T.S. Eliot

Eliot challenges us to push beyond our perceived limits through risk and adventure. This quote implies that true discovery and achievement lie beyond the boundaries of comfort and certainty. It's an encouragement to test our limits, as only by daring to venture beyond them can we truly realize our full potential.

6. "The real voyage of discovery consists not in seeking new landscapes, but in having new eyes." - Marcel Proust

Proust offers a profound insight into exploration, suggesting that true discovery comes from seeing the world differently rather than merely changing our physical location. This quote emphasizes that shifts in perspective and openness to new experiences can transform the familiar into the extraordinary. It's a reminder that adventure and exploration are as much about internal growth as they are about external journeys.

7. "Exploration is really the essence of the human spirit." - Frank Borman

Borman, an astronaut, speaks to the innate human drive to explore and discover. This quote reflects the idea that exploration is fundamental to human nature, driving us to seek out new knowledge, challenge ourselves, and push the boundaries of what is known. It's a testament to the curiosity and resilience that define the human experience.

Frank Frederick Borman II was an American United States Air Force colonel, aeronautical engineer, NASA astronaut, test pilot, and businessman.

Born: 1928, Gary, IN

Died: November 7, 2023

8. "Life is either a daring adventure or nothing at all." - Helen Keller

Keller, despite her physical limitations, advocates for a life lived boldly and without fear. This quote suggests that embracing adventure and taking risks are essential to experiencing life fully. It highlights the choice between seeking out the richness of experience or accepting a more limited existence, urging us to choose the former.

9. "Do not follow where the path may lead. Go instead where there is no path and leave a trail." - Ralph Waldo Emerson

Emerson encourages originality and pioneering spirit in exploration. This quote inspires us to forge our own paths and make unique discoveries rather than treading along well-worn routes. It's an advocacy for innovation and leadership in exploration, emphasizing the impact of charting new courses for others to follow.

10. "Man cannot discover new oceans unless he has the courage to lose sight of the shore." - André Gide

Gide underscores the necessity of courage in the pursuit of discovery. This quote metaphorically suggests that to achieve significant breakthroughs or experiences, we must be willing to leave behind the familiar and venture into the unknown. It highlights the inherent risks and fears associated with exploration but frames them as essential to gaining new insights and experiences.

André Paul Guillaume Gide was a French author whose writings spanned a wide variety of styles and topics. He was awarded the 1947 Nobel Prize in Literature. Gide's career ranged from his beginnings in the symbolist movement, to criticizing imperialism between the two World Wars.

Born: November 22, 1869, Paris, France

Died: February 19, 1951

Chapter 20. 'Forgiveness and letting go' Quotes

Forgiveness and letting go are powerful processes that lead to healing and personal growth. They require strength and compassion, both towards ourselves and others.

These quotes on forgiveness and letting go remind us of the healing power of releasing past hurts and resentments. They emphasize that forgiveness is a profound act of strength and liberation that not only frees.

Here are some of the best quotes on forgiveness and letting go, with explanations to delve into their profound meanings:

1. "The weak can never forgive. Forgiveness is the attribute of the strong." - Mahatma Gandhi

Gandhi suggests that forgiveness requires immense strength, contrary to the common perception that it is a sign of weakness. This quote emphasizes that it takes a strong person to forgive, as it involves overcoming pride, anger, and resentment to make peace with the past. Forgiveness, in this light, is seen as a powerful act of courage and strength.

2. "To forgive is to set a prisoner free and discover that the prisoner was you." - Lewis B. Smedes

Smedes highlights the liberating effect of forgiveness on the forgiver. This quote suggests that holding onto anger and grudges traps us in a state of suffering and that through forgiveness, we free ourselves from this self-imposed prison. Forgiveness is portrayed as a crucial step towards personal freedom and peace.

3. "Letting go means coming to the realization that some people are a part of your history, but not a part of your destiny." - Steve Maraboli

Maraboli speaks to the importance of recognizing when to move on from relationships that no longer contribute to our growth. This quote suggests that while certain people may play significant roles in our past, they may not necessarily fit into our future. Letting go is about understanding and accepting that our paths may diverge, allowing us to focus on our personal journey and destiny.

Dr. Steve Maraboli is a life-changing Speaker, bestselling Author, and Behavioral Science Academic. His empowering and insightful words have been shared and published throughout the world in more than 25 languages. .

Born: 1975 , Port Washington, NY

4. "Forgiveness does not change the past, but it does enlarge the future." - Paul Boese

Boese points out that while forgiveness cannot undo what has been done, it opens the possibility for personal growth and expanded opportunities in the future. This quote emphasizes that forgiveness is not about altering historical events but about transforming our relationship to them, thereby allowing us to move forward with a lighter heart and a broader perspective.

5. "Resentment is like drinking poison and then hoping it will kill your enemies." - Nelson Mandela

Mandela vividly illustrates the self-destructive nature of holding onto resentment. This quote suggests that resentment harms us more than it affects those we resent, likening it to self-poisoning. It underscores the importance of letting go of bitterness, not for the sake of others, but for our own well-being.

6. "Letting go does not mean you stop caring. It means you stop trying to force others to." - Mandy Hale

Hale clarifies that letting go of someone or something is not an act of indifference but an acceptance of the limits of our control over others' feelings and actions. This quote highlights the distinction between caring for someone and attempting to manipulate their feelings or behaviors, advocating for a release of the latter as a path to genuine peace and respect.

7. "Forgiveness is not about forgetting. It is about letting go of another person's throat." - William Paul Young

Young uses a powerful metaphor to describe forgiveness as a release of the grip of blame and anger we hold against someone. This quote challenges the common misconception that forgiveness involves forgetting what happened. Instead, it presents forgiveness as a conscious choice to let go of resentment and the desire for retribution, freeing both the forgiver and the forgiven from the cycle of anger.

8. "Forgiveness is the fragrance that the violet sheds on the heel that has crushed it." - Mark Twain

Twain poetically portrays forgiveness as an act of grace and beauty, likening it to a violet that releases its fragrance even when crushed. This quote suggests that forgiveness is a noble response to injury or insult, offering kindness and compassion in return for harm. It elevates forgiveness to an act of moral and spiritual generosity.

9. "Let go of the belief that the past could have been any different." - Oprah Winfrey

Oprah encourages acceptance of the past as it is, challenging the futile longing for a different past. This quote underscores the importance of letting go of fantasies about how things could have been, advocating for a peaceful acceptance of reality. It points to the understanding that embracing the past, with its imperfections, is crucial for moving forward unburdened.

Chapter 21. Empathy and compassion Quotes

Empathy and compassion are fundamental to human connection, enabling us to understand and share the feelings of others and act with kindness and consideration.

Here are some of the best quotes on empathy and compassion, each followed by a comprehensive explanation to explore their deeper significance:

1."Empathy is seeing with the eyes of another, listening with the ears of another, and feeling with the heart of another." - Alfred Adler

Adler defines empathy as the ability to fully immerse oneself in another's experience, adopting their perspective both emotionally and perceptually. This quote underscores the multi-dimensional nature of empathy, involving not just emotional resonance but a conscious effort to understand others' viewpoints and feelings. It highlights empathy as a holistic approach to understanding the human condition, fostering deeper connections and compassion.

2. "Compassion is the radicalism of our time." - Dalai Lama

The Dalai Lama elevates compassion to a powerful force for change, labeling it as radical in its ability to transform society. This quote challenges us to view compassion not as a passive or soft virtue but as an active, courageous stance against indifference and cruelty. It positions compassion as essential for addressing the world's suffering and injustices, suggesting that empathy and kindness can revolutionize how we interact with one another and the planet.

3. "The only way to understand someone is to love them without hope." - Walter Benjamin

Benjamin suggests that true understanding and empathy come from unconditional love, free from expectations or desires for reciprocity. This quote speaks to the selfless nature of genuine compassion, where understanding and acceptance are offered freely, without attachment to outcomes. It emphasizes love as the foundation for deep empathy, encouraging us to embrace others as they are.

Walter Bendix Schönflies Benjamin was a German Jewish philosopher, cultural critic, media theorist, and essayist.

Born: July 15, 1892, Berlin, Germany

Died: September 26, 1940

4. "We think we listen, but very rarely do we listen with real understanding, true empathy. Yet listening, of this very special kind, is one of the most potent forces for change that I know." - Carl Rogers

Rogers, a pioneering psychologist, highlights the rarity and power of listening with true empathy. This quote emphasizes that genuine understanding requires more than just hearing words; it involves a deep engagement with and validation of another's feelings and experiences. Rogers points out the transformative potential of empathetic listening, both for personal relationships and broader societal healing.

5. "If you want others to be happy, practice compassion. If you want to be happy, practice compassion." - Dalai Lama

The Dalai Lama presents compassion as a key to happiness, both for ourselves and others. This quote suggests that compassion is not just an outwardly directed virtue but also a source of personal fulfillment. It highlights the reciprocal nature of kindness, where the act of nurturing others' well-being contributes to our own.

6. "You never really understand a person until you consider things from his point of view... Until you climb into his skin and walk around in it." - Harper Lee, from "To Kill a Mockingbird"

Through the character Atticus Finch, Harper Lee advocates for deep empathy as a means of understanding others. This quote challenges us to go beyond superficial judgments, inviting us to truly immerse ourselves in another's life and perspective. It's a call to practice empathy by seeking to experience the world as others do, fostering greater understanding and compassion.

7. "Kindness begins with the understanding that we all struggle." - Charles Glassman

Glassman identifies a common ground for compassion: the universal experience of struggle. This quote suggests that kindness is rooted in recognizing our shared vulnerabilities and challenges. By acknowledging that everyone faces hardships, we can approach others with greater empathy and support.

8. "Compassion hurts. When you feel connected to everything, you also feel responsible for everything. And you cannot turn away. Your destiny is bound with the destinies of others. You must either learn to carry the Universe or be crushed by it." - Andrew Boyd

Boyd delves into the weight of true compassion, highlighting its expansive nature and the sense of responsibility it entails. This quote speaks to the depth of feeling involved in genuine empathy, where the boundaries between self and others blur. It emphasizes that compassion demands strength and the willingness to engage with the pain of the world, seeing it as intertwined with our own fate.

9. "The greatest cruelty is our casual blindness to the despair of others." – Unknown

This quote criticizes indifference as a profound form of cruelty, pointing out the harm caused by ignoring others' suffering. It underscores the importance of empathy in recognizing and responding to the pain around us, suggesting that a failure to acknowledge others' struggles contributes to their continuation.

10. "Do not wait for leaders; do it alone, person to person." - Mother Teresa

Mother Teresa encourages individual action rooted in compassion and empathy, rather than relying on leaders or institutions to instigate change. This quote inspires personal responsibility for fostering kindness and understanding on a one-to-one basis, highlighting the power of direct, personal interactions in making.

Chapter 22. Leadership & Influence Quotes

Leadership and influence are critical in guiding others toward achieving common goals and inspiring positive change.

These following quotes on leadership and influence shed light on the nuanced and multifaceted nature of leading effectively. They remind us that true leadership is about empowering others, acting with integrity, and transforming visions into realities through a balanced approach of strength and compassion.

1 "The greatest leader is not necessarily the one who does the greatest things. He is the one that gets the people to do the greatest things." - Ronald Reagan

Reagan's quote emphasizes that effective leadership is not about personal achievements, but about empowering and motivating others to achieve greatness. It highlights the role of a leader as a facilitator of talent and effort within a team, suggesting that the true measure of leadership is in the collective success fostered through guidance and inspiration.

2. "Leadership is not about being in charge. It is about taking care of those in your charge." - Simon Sinek

Simon Sinek shifts the focus of leadership from authority to responsibility, suggesting that true leadership involves nurturing and protecting those you lead. This quote challenges traditional views of leadership as a position of power, instead framing it as a role of service and stewardship, emphasizing the leader's duty to support and ensure the well-being of their team.

3. "To handle yourself, use your head; to handle others, use your heart." - Eleanor Roosevelt

Roosevelt advises that intellectual strategies are best for managing oneself, while emotional intelligence is crucial in dealing with others. This quote underscores the importance of empathy, compassion, and understanding in leadership, highlighting that connecting with others on an emotional level is key to effective influence and guidance.

Eleanor Roosevelt (1884–1962) was an American political figure, diplomat, and activist who became one of the most influential First Ladies in U.S. history while her husband, Franklin D. Roosevelt, served as President from 1933 to 1945. Born Anna Eleanor Roosevelt, she transformed the traditionally ceremonial role of the First Lady by her active participation in American politics and her involvement in social issues.

4. "The function of leadership is to produce more leaders, not more followers." - Ralph Nader

Nader's quote suggests that the ultimate goal of leadership should be to empower others to become leaders themselves. It emphasizes the idea of leadership as a transformative process that encourages independence, critical thinking, and initiative, rather than merely cultivating obedience and passivity.

5. "Before you are a leader, success is all about growing yourself. When you become a leader, success is all about growing others." - Jack Welch

Welch distinguishes between personal success and leadership success, highlighting that leadership involves facilitating the growth and development of others. This quote reflects the transition from self-focused improvement to a broader focus on mentoring, teaching, and empowering others as a core element of leadership.

6. "People buy into the leader before they buy into the vision." - John C. Maxwell

Maxwell points out that the credibility and character of a leader are foundational to gaining the trust and commitment of their followers. This quote emphasizes that people are more likely to embrace and pursue a vision if they respect and believe in the person who presents it, underscoring the importance of personal integrity and authenticity in leadership.

7. "Leadership is the capacity to translate vision into reality." - Warren Bennis

Bennis defines leadership as the ability to turn ideas and visions into tangible outcomes. This quote suggests that effective leaders are those who cannot only envision a better future but also mobilize resources, inspire action, and implement strategies to make that vision come true.

Warren Gamaliel Bennis was an American scholar, organizational consultant and author, widely regarded as a pioneer of the contemporary field of Leadership studies.

Born: March 8, 1925, New York, NY

Died: July 31, 2014

8. "Do not follow where the path may lead. Go instead where there is no path and leave a trail." - Ralph Waldo Emerson

Emerson encourages originality and pioneering in leadership, advocating for creating one's own path rather than conforming to established routes. This quote inspires leaders to innovate, challenge the status quo, and set new precedents, highlighting the value of trailblazing and setting new benchmarks for others to follow.

9. "A leader is best when people barely know he exists, when his work is done, his aim fulfilled, they will say: we did it ourselves." - Lao Tzu

Lao Tzu presents a model of leadership that is subtle yet profoundly impactful, suggesting that the most effective leaders are those who guide their teams in such a way that the team feels a sense of ownership and accomplishment. This quote emphasizes leadership as an art of empowerment and facilitation, where the leader's influence is seamlessly integrated into the collective effort.

10. "The challenge of leadership is to be strong, but not rude; be kind, but not weak; be bold, but not a bully; be thoughtful, but not lazy; be humble, but not timid; be proud, but not arrogant; have humor, but without folly." - Jim Rohn

Rohn articulates the delicate balance required in effective leadership, listing dualities that leaders must navigate. This quote underscores the complexity of leadership, emphasizing that it involves a harmonious blend of strength and sensitivity, assertiveness and empathy, confidence and humility.

Emanuel James Rohn, professionally known as Jim Rohn, was an American entrepreneur, author and motivational speaker. He has written numerous books, like "How to obtain wealth and happiness".

Born: September 17, 1930, Yakima, WA

Died: December 5, 2009

Chapter 23. Innovation & creativity Quotes

Innovation and creativity are the lifeblood of progress and transformation in society, business, and personal development. They involve thinking outside the box, challenging conventional wisdom, and daring to imagine new possibilities.

These quotes inspire us to embrace creativity and innovation as essential tools for leadership, progress, and personal growth. They remind us that pushing boundaries, challenging the status quo, and imagining new possibilities are not just acts of individual expression but fundamental drivers of change and advancement in every field of human endeavor.

Here are some of the best quotes on innovation and creativity, each accompanied by an in-depth explanation to explore their profound implications:

1. "Innovation distinguishes between a leader and a follower." - Steve Jobs

Jobs asserts that the capacity to innovate sets leaders apart from followers. This quote underscores the idea that true leaders are those who do not just adapt to the world as it is but seek to change it through novel ideas and approaches. Innovation, in this sense, is the hallmark of visionary thinking and leadership.

2. "Creativity is thinking up new things. Innovation is doing new things." - Theodore Levitt

Levitt makes a critical distinction between creativity and innovation. Creativity involves the generation of new ideas, while innovation refers to the practical application of those ideas into actionable changes or new products. This quote highlights the complementary relationship between the two: creativity fuels innovation, and innovation brings creative ideas to life.

Theodore Levitt was a German-born American economist and a professor at the Harvard Business School. He was editor of the Harvard Business Review, noted for increasing the Review's circulation and popularizing the term globalization.

Born: March 1, 1925, Vollmerz, Schlüchtern, Germany

Died: June 28, 2006

3. "The only way to discover the limits of the possible is to go beyond them into the impossible." - Arthur C. Clarke

Clarke challenges us to push beyond the boundaries of what is currently known to discover what could be possible. This quote encapsulates the essence of innovation and creativity, which often require venturing into uncharted territory and redefining the parameters of possibility.

4. "Do not fear mistakes. There are none." - Miles Davis

Davis encourages a fearless approach to creativity and innovation, suggesting that what might initially appear as mistakes are, in fact, essential steps in the creative process. This quote advocates for a mindset that views setbacks not as failures but as opportunities for learning and growth, essential for fostering true innovation.

5. "If you always do what you always did, you will always get what you always got." - Albert Einstein

Einstein highlights the necessity of change for achieving different outcomes. This quote underscores the importance of breaking away from routine and conventional methods to achieve breakthroughs and innovations. It suggests that creativity requires stepping out of comfort zones and experimenting with new approaches.

6. "The true sign of intelligence is not knowledge but imagination." - Albert Einstein

Einstein elevates imagination above knowledge as the key indicator of intelligence. This quote suggests that while knowledge is important, the ability to think creatively and imagine new possibilities is what drives innovation and progress. Imagination is presented as the source of original ideas and solutions.

7. "It is not the strongest of the species that survive, nor the most intelligent, but the one most responsive to change." - Charles Darwin

Darwin's observation about natural selection can also be applied to the context of innovation and creativity. This quote suggests that adaptability and responsiveness to change are key to survival and success, whether in nature or in the business world. It highlights the importance of being open to new ideas and willing to innovate in response to evolving circumstances.

Charles Robert Darwin was an English naturalist, geologist and biologist, widely known for his contributions to evolutionary biology. His proposition that all species of life have descended from a common ancestor is now generally accepted and considered a fundamental concept in science.

Born: February 12, 1809, The Mount House, Shrewsbury, United Kingdom

Died: April 19, 1882

8. "Creativity is contagious, pass it on." - Albert Einstein

Einstein posits that creativity has a ripple effect, inspiring those it touches to think and act creatively as well. This quote emphasizes the social aspect of creativity, suggesting that sharing creative ideas and approaches can foster a culture of innovation and collective progress.

9. "Innovation is the calling card of the future." - Anna Eshoo

Eshoo positions innovation as a forward-looking act, essential for shaping the future. This quote suggests that the willingness to innovate is what prepares individuals and societies to meet and create what lies ahead. It frames innovation as not just a response to current challenges but as a proactive step towards building the future.

10. "The best way to predict the future is to invent it." - Alan Kay

Kay emphasizes the proactive role of innovation and creativity in shaping the future. Instead of passively trying to forecast what might happen, this quote encourages taking an active role in creating the future through imaginative and innovative efforts. It highlights the power of human agency in designing tomorrow's world.

Alan Curtis Kay is an American computer scientist best known for his pioneering work on object-oriented programming and windowing graphical user interface design. At Xerox PARC he led the design and development of the first modern windowed computer desktop interface.

Born: 1940 (age 83 years), Springfield, MA

Chapter 24. Peace and nonviolence quotes

Peace and nonviolence are fundamental principles that seek to transform society through understanding, compassion, and the rejection of violence as a means to resolve conflict.

These quotes on peace and nonviolence remind us of the ethical and practical imperative to seek understanding, practice empathy, and engage in positive actions as the paths to resolving conflict and building a more harmonious world. They highlight the interconnectedness of peace, freedom, and mutual respect.

Here are some of the best quotes on peace and nonviolence, each followed by a detailed explanation to illuminate their depth and significance:

1 "Peace cannot be kept by force; it can only be achieved by understanding." - Albert Einstein

Einstein suggests that true peace is not a state that can be imposed through coercion or military strength. Instead, it is a condition that emerges from mutual understanding and dialogue. This quote highlights the necessity of empathy, communication, and cooperation as foundations for lasting peace, emphasizing that understanding the perspectives and needs of others is key to resolving conflicts.

2. "Nonviolence is the first article of my faith. It is also the last article of my creed." - Mahatma Gandhi

Gandhi, a staunch advocate for nonviolence, expresses his unwavering commitment to nonviolent principles as both a personal belief and a guiding philosophy. This quote underscores nonviolence not merely as a strategy but as a fundamental value that informs all actions and decisions. It reflects the deep conviction that nonviolence is the most ethical and effective way to achieve social and political change.

3."There is no way to peace; peace is the way." - A.J. Muste

Muste's quote is a profound assertion that peace itself is the path to resolving conflict, rather than a distant goal to be reached through other means. This statement challenges the notion of using violence or aggression as strategies for achieving peace, advocating instead for peace to be practiced in every action and interaction as the only true route to a peaceful society.

Abraham Johannes Muste, usually cited as A. J. Muste, was a Dutch-born American clergyman and political activist. He is best remembered for his work in the labor movement, pacifist movement, antiwar movement, and civil rights movement.

Born: January 8, 1885, Zierikzee, Netherlands

Died: February 11, 1967

4. "Darkness cannot drive out darkness; only light can do that. Hate cannot drive out hate; only love can do that." - Martin Luther King Jr.

King highlights the ineffectiveness of responding to negativity with more negativity. This quote emphasizes the transformative power of positive forces such as love and light to overcome darkness and hate. It suggests that adopting attitudes of compassion, understanding, and forgiveness are essential in healing divisions and fostering peace.

5. "Peace is not merely a distant goal that we seek, but a means by which we arrive at that goal." - Martin Luther King Jr.

Here, King articulates that peace is both an end and a means, suggesting that peaceful methods should be employed in the pursuit of peace itself. This quote encourages the practice of peace in everyday actions and decisions, emphasizing that the manner in which we seek peace is as important as the achievement of peace itself.

6. "An eye for an eye only ends up making the whole world blind." - Mahatma Gandhi

Gandhi critiques the principle of retaliation or revenge, arguing that responding to violence with violence only perpetuates a cycle of harm that ultimately leads to collective suffering. This quote advocates for breaking the cycle of aggression through forgiveness and nonviolent resistance, highlighting the futility and destructiveness of revenge.

7. "The more we sweat in peace, the less we bleed in war." - Vijaya Lakshmi Pandit

Pandit emphasizes the importance of proactive efforts toward peace to prevent the outbreak of conflict. This quote suggests that investing time and resources in peacebuilding activities, such as diplomacy, education, and social justice, can significantly reduce the likelihood and severity of war. It underscores the value of preparation and prevention in maintaining peace.

Vijaya Lakshmi Pandit was an Indian freedom fighter, diplomat and politician. She served as the 8th President of the United Nations General Assembly from 1953 to 1954, the first woman appointed to either post.

Born: August 18, 1900, Prayagraj, India

Died: December 1, 1990

8. "For to be free is not merely to cast off one's chains, but to live in a way that respects and enhances the freedom of others." - Nelson Mandela

Mandela connects the concept of personal freedom to the broader context of peace and nonviolence, suggesting that true freedom involves living in harmony with and respecting the rights of others. This quote emphasizes that individual liberty should not infringe upon the freedom of others but should contribute to a peaceful, equitable society where all can thrive.

9. "You cannot shake hands with a clenched fist." - Indira Gandhi

Gandhi metaphorically speaks to the impossibility of achieving peace and reconciliation without first letting go of aggression and hostility. This quote underscores the need for openness, willingness to dialogue, and mutual respect as prerequisites for peace, emphasizing that genuine peace requires both sides to disarm, literally and figuratively.

10. "Peace begins with a smile." - Mother Teresa

Mother Teresa highlights the simplicity of starting the journey toward peace with a simple, kind gesture. This quote suggests that even small acts of kindness and goodwill can contribute to a more peaceful world. It underscores the power of compassion and human connection as foundational elements in fostering peace.

Mary Teresa Bojaxhiu MC, better known as Mother Teresa, was an Albanian-Indian Catholic nun and the founder of the Missionaries of Charity. Born in Skopje, then part of the Ottoman Empire, at the age of 18 she moved to Ireland and later to India, where she lived most of her life.

Born: August 26, 1910, Skopje, North Macedonia

Died: September 5, 1997

Chapter 25. Self-discovery Quotes

Self-discovery is a journey into understanding one's own identity, desires, and purpose. It involves introspection, confronting fears, and embracing both strengths and vulnerabilities.

These quotes on self-discovery remind us that the journey to knowing oneself is rich, challenging, and ultimately rewarding.

Here are some of the best quotes on self-discovery, each followed by a detailed explanation to explore their profound meanings:

1. "The only journey is the journey within." - Rainer Maria Rilke

Rilke emphasizes that the most significant exploration we can undertake is into our own selves. This quote suggests that true understanding and growth come from introspection and self-awareness, not from external adventures or acquisitions. It highlights the depth and complexity of the human psyche and the value of engaging with our inner world to find meaning and purpose.

2. "Knowing yourself is the beginning of all wisdom." – Aristotle

Aristotle posits that self-knowledge is the foundation of wisdom. This quote underscores the idea that understanding our own nature, motivations, and desires is essential for making wise decisions and living a fulfilling life. It suggests that self-awareness is the first step in navigating the complexities of life with insight and discernment.

3. "Man cannot discover new oceans unless he has the courage to lose sight of the shore." - André Gide

While Gide's quote can be interpreted in the context of physical exploration, it also metaphorically speaks to the process of self-discovery. It suggests that venturing into the unknown aspects of our own psyche requires bravery and a willingness to leave behind familiar but limiting beliefs or identities. This quote highlights the necessity of courage and openness in the pursuit of deeper self-understanding and personal growth.

André Paul Guillaume Gide was a French author whose writings spanned a wide variety of styles and topics. He was awarded the 1947 Nobel Prize in Literature. Gide's career ranged from his beginnings in the symbolist movement, to criticizing imperialism between the two World Wars.

Born: November 22, 1869, Paris, France

Died: February 19, 1951

4. "To find yourself, think for yourself." - Socrates

Socrates champions the importance of independent thought in the journey of self-discovery. This quote encourages us to question societal norms and conventions and to form our own beliefs and values. It suggests that authentic self-knowledge arises from critical thinking and self-reliance, rather than uncritically adopting the views of others.

5. "Your work is to discover your world and then with all your heart give yourself to it." – Buddha

Buddha advises us to engage deeply with the process of self-discovery and to devote ourselves fully to living according to our discoveries. This quote speaks to the idea of aligning one's actions with one's true nature and calling, suggesting that fulfillment comes from a wholehearted commitment to living authentically based on our personal understanding and values.

6. "The privilege of a lifetime is to become who you truly are." - Carl Jung

Jung reflects on the profound opportunity and challenge of realizing one's true self. This quote underscores the journey of self-discovery as a privilege that allows us to live as our most authentic selves. It highlights the process of individuation—the development of the individual from undifferentiated mass of societal expectations to a fully realized unique person—as a key task of a fulfilled life.

7. "The best way to find yourself is to lose yourself in the service of others." - Mahatma Gandhi

Gandhi presents a paradoxical approach to self-discovery, suggesting that we can understand ourselves better through selflessness and serving others. This quote emphasizes that empathy, compassion, and altruism can be pathways to understanding our own capacities, values, and purpose, revealing aspects of ourselves that might remain hidden in purely self-centered pursuits.

8. "I can teach anybody how to get what they want out of life. The problem is that I can't find anybody who can tell me what they want." - Mark Twain

Twain humorously points out a common dilemma in self-discovery: identifying our true desires. This quote suggests that while achieving goals may be straightforward, the real challenge lies in understanding ourselves well enough to know what we genuinely want from life. It emphasizes the importance of clarity in self-knowledge as a precursor to fulfillment.

Samuel Langhorne Clemens, known by the pen name Mark Twain, was an American writer, humorist, essayist, entrepreneur, publisher and lecturer. He was praised as the "greatest humorist the United States has produced," with William Faulkner calling him "the father of American literature."

Born: November 30, 1835, Florida, MO

Died: April 21, 1910

9. "What you discover on your own is always more exciting than what someone else discovers for you - it's like the marriage between romantic love and an arranged marriage." - Terrence Rafferty

Rafferty compares the joy of self-discovery to the thrill of romantic love, suggesting that insights we uncover through our own efforts are more meaningful and exhilarating than those handed to us by others. This quote highlights the value of personal exploration and the excitement that comes from actively engaging in the journey of self-understanding.

10. "There are three things extremely hard: steel, a diamond, and to know oneself." - Benjamin Franklin

Franklin likens self-knowledge to the hardness of steel and diamonds, suggesting that self-discovery is among the most challenging endeavors one can undertake. This quote underscores the complexity of the human psyche and the effort required to achieve true self-awareness, placing the quest for self-knowledge as a formidable but worthy pursuit.

11. "Man cannot find himself without first achieving a separation from himself." - Erich Fromm

Fromm speaks to the paradox of self-discovery, suggesting that one must somehow step outside of oneself to gain a true understanding of one's nature. This quote highlights the complexity of self-awareness, indicating that detachment or a shift in perspective is necessary to see oneself clearly and objectively.

12. "Everything that irritates us about others can lead us to an understanding of ourselves." - Carl Jung

Jung points out that our reactions to others serve as mirrors for our own inner world. This quote suggests that interpersonal conflicts and annoyances offer valuable opportunities for self-reflection, revealing aspects of ourselves that we may need to confront or understand better. It highlights the role of external relationships in the journey of self-discovery, showing how they can illuminate our own patterns, biases, and areas for growth.

Carl Gustav Jung was a Swiss psychiatrist and psychoanalyst who founded analytical psychology. He was a prolific author, illustrator, and correspondent, and a complex and controversial character, presumably best known through his "autobiography" Memories, Dreams, Reflections.

Born: July 26, 1875, Kesswil, Switzerland

Died: June 6, 1961

Chapter 26. Humility and modesty Quotes

Humility and modesty are virtues that reflect a grounded and realistic sense of one's abilities and achievements, coupled with a respectful and considerate attitude towards others.

These quotes will reveal the complexity and richness of these virtues, illustrating how they contribute to personal authenticity, ethical behavior, and meaningful social interactions. They remind us that true greatness and nobility lie in recognizing our limitations, focusing on self-improvement, and valuing others with respect and consideration.

Here are some of the best quotes on humility and modesty, each followed by an in-depth explanation to explore their deeper meanings:

1 "Humility is not thinking less of yourself but thinking of yourself less." - C.S. Lewis

Lewis provides a nuanced definition of humility, distinguishing it from low self-esteem. This quote suggests that humility involves shifting focus away from oneself and prioritizing the needs and concerns of others. It highlights that being humble doesn't mean undervaluing oneself, but rather, cultivating a selfless perspective that values others' contributions and well-being.

2. "The only wisdom we can hope to acquire is the wisdom of humility." - T.S. Eliot

Eliot elevates humility to the highest form of wisdom, suggesting that recognizing the limits of our knowledge and understanding is foundational to true insight. This quote points to humility as a virtue that opens us up to learning and growth, as it acknowledges that there is always more to know and understand beyond our current perspective.

3. "Pride makes us artificial and humility makes us real." - Thomas Merton

Merton contrasts pride with humility, arguing that pride leads to a constructed and false sense of self, while humility allows us to be authentic and genuine. This quote emphasizes that humility connects us with our true nature and with others in a sincere and honest way, fostering genuine relationships and self-acceptance.

Thomas Merton OCSO was an American Trappist monk, writer, theologian, mystic, poet, social activist and scholar of comparative religion. On May 26, 1949, he was ordained to the Catholic priesthood and given the name "Father Louis".

Born: January 31, 1915, Prades, France

Died: December 10, 1968

4. "Modesty is the gentle art of enhancing your charm by pretending not to be aware of it." - Oliver Herford

Herford humorously describes modesty as an art form that involves downplaying one's attributes or achievements to appear more appealing. This quote highlights modesty as a social virtue that endears individuals to others by not overtly seeking admiration or attention, thereby maintaining a gracious and likable demeanor.

5. "A great man is always willing to be little." - Ralph Waldo Emerson

Emerson suggests that greatness includes the willingness to occupy a humble position or status when necessary. This quote emphasizes that individuals who achieve greatness are those who do not cling to their accomplishments or demand recognition, but instead, demonstrate humility and a readiness to serve others or the greater good.

6. "Humility is the solid foundation of all virtues." – Confucius

Confucius positions humility as the cornerstone upon which all other virtues are built. This quote implies that without humility, other positive qualities lack a firm grounding. Humility is presented as essential for the development and expression of virtues such as compassion, patience, and generosity, as it keeps ego in check and aligns one's actions with moral integrity.

7. "There is nothing noble in being superior to your fellow man; true nobility is being superior to your former self." - Ernest Hemingway

Hemingway shifts the focus of nobility from comparison with others to personal self-improvement. This quote suggests that true greatness lies in overcoming our own limitations and bettering ourselves, rather than outshining others. It underscores humility and modesty as virtues that recognize personal growth as the most meaningful measure of success.

Ernest Miller Hemingway was an American novelist, short-story writer and journalist. He is known for the economical, understated style that significantly influenced later 20th-century writers, who admired his adventurous lifestyle and public image.

Born: July 21, 1899, Oak Park, IL

Died: July 2, 1961

8. "Modesty is the color of virtue." – Diogenes

Diogenes metaphorically attributes modesty as the defining characteristic of virtue, suggesting that it colors and shapes the essence of ethical behavior. This quote highlights modesty as an attribute that complements and enhances virtue, making it more genuine and admirable.

9. "Humility, that low, sweet root, from which all heavenly virtues shoot." - Thomas Moore

Moore poetically describes humility as the foundational quality from which all other virtues emerge. This quote likens humility to a root that nurtures and supports the growth of other positive traits, emphasizing its fundamental role in the cultivation of a virtuous character.

Thomas Moore, also known as Tom Moore, was an Irish writer, poet, and lyricist celebrated for his Irish Melodies. His setting of English-language verse to old Irish tunes marked the transition in popular Irish culture from Irish to English.

Born: May 28, 1779, Dublin, Ireland

Died: February 25, 1852

Chapter 27. Sex Quotes

1.God created sex. Priests created marriage. - Voltaire

The statement "God created sex. Priests created marriage." is a simplistic yet thought-provoking assertion that touches upon the origins of human sexual relationships and the institution of marriage. Here's an exploration of its underlying meanings:

-"God created sex" refers to the belief in many religious and spiritual traditions that human sexuality is a natural, divinely instituted aspect of human existence. From this perspective, sex is seen as a gift from the divine, intended for procreation, expression of love, and the deepening of intimate bonds between partners. It underscores the idea that sexuality is an integral, innate part of being human, imbued with potential for deep connection, pleasure, and the continuation of life.

-"Priests created marriage" points to the historical development of marriage as a social, legal, and religious institution. While not solely the domain of priests or any single religious tradition, marriage has been shaped significantly by religious practices, doctrines, and authority figures over millennia. This part of the statement highlights the role of religious institutions in codifying, regulating, and sanctifying marital relationships, often with specific rules, rituals, and expectations. It suggests that marriage, as a formal institution, is a human-made construct, developed to organize, legitimize, and sanctify relationships in the eyes of the community and the divine.

The contrast between the two assertions draws attention to the distinction between the natural, intrinsic aspects of human sexuality and the socially constructed, institutional aspects of marital relationships. It invites reflection on how different cultures, religions, and societies have navigated the complexities of sexual relationships and the structures they've created to manage and understand those relationships.

While the statement is somewhat reductive, ignoring the nuanced views of different faiths and cultures regarding sex and marriage, it serves as a starting point for discussion on the interplay between natural human impulses and the social, religious, and legal frameworks constructed around them.

2. Sex: the pleasure is momentary, the position ridiculous, and the expense damnable. — Lord Chesterfield

The quote attributed to Lord Chesterfield reflects a cynical and humorous view on sexual relations. Philip Stanhope, the 4th Earl of Chesterfield, was known for his wit and the letters he wrote to his son, offering advice on a variety of subjects, including social etiquette and personal conduct.

The quote encapsulates a skeptical view of sexual pursuits, emphasizing their temporary pleasure, inherent awkwardness, and potential for negative consequences. It reflects Chesterfield's style of imparting wisdom through sharp wit and a realistic assessment of human behaviors and desires. While the tone is humorous, it also invites reflection on the complexities and contradictions of human sexuality and relationships.

3. Love is a matter of chemistry, but sex is a matter of physics. — Alexandre Dumas

This quote, often attributed to Alexandre Dumas, juxtaposes the abstract, emotional aspects of love with the tangible, physical aspects of sex, using the disciplines of chemistry and physics as metaphors to highlight their differences. While the authenticity of this attribution to Dumas may be questionable, as it doesn't appear in his well-documented writings and could reflect a popular misattribution or an apocryphal status, the quote itself offers a witty and insightful observation on the nature of romantic and sexual human relationships. Let's break it down:

-**"Love is a matter of chemistry"**: This part of the quote suggests that love involves complex emotional and psychological interactions, much like the reactions and bonds formed in chemical processes. Chemistry here symbolizes the invisible, intangible connections that draw people together, creating feelings of attraction, attachment, and affection. It emphasizes that love is about the compatibility and interaction between different personalities, moods, and emotions, leading to a unique and often inexplicable bond.

-**"Sex is a matter of physics"**: In contrast, this part of the quote highlights the physical and tangible nature of sex, governed by the laws of physics—motion, forces, and energy. It points to the physical actions and reactions, the bodily connections, and the mechanics of sexual intercourse. Here, sex is viewed in terms of physical compatibility, the act itself, and the biological responses it invokes, independent of the emotional or psychological aspects that may accompany it.

The charm of the quote lies in its clever use of scientific disciplines as metaphors to differentiate between the emotional/psychological aspects of love and the physical/biological aspects of sex. It humorously but effectively captures the dichotomy between the emotional bonds that can form without physical contact (chemistry) and the physical interactions that can occur without emotional bonds (physics).

While love and sex are often interconnected in human relationships, this quote succinctly encapsulates the distinction between them, highlighting how one can be deeply complex and emotional, while the other can be straightforwardly physical. It also serves as a reminder of the multifaceted nature of human relationships, which can involve a blend of both these elements, each governed by its own set of rules and dynamics.

4. Everything in the world is about sex except sex. Sex is about power. — Oscar Wilde

The quote delves into the complex interplay between sexuality, societal norms, and power dynamics. Wilde, known for his wit and insight into human nature, presents a provocative statement that invites reflection on the underlying motivations and implications of sexual relationships and behaviors.

"Everything in the world is about sex": This first part suggests that sexual desire and attraction underpin much of human behavior and societal structures, even when they appear unrelated to sexuality on the surface. Wilde implies that the pursuit of sex, or the appeal to sexual desires, influences a wide range of human activities, from art and literature to politics and economics. This perspective aligns with Freudian theories that see sexuality as a driving force in human life, shaping our motivations and actions in often unconscious ways.

"except sex": The twist in Wilde's statement comes with the assertion that sex itself, when scrutinized, transcends mere physical desire or procreation. By distinguishing sex from its apparent biological and emotional motivations, Wilde opens the door to a deeper discussion on what truly lies at the heart of sexual encounters and relationships.

"Sex is about power": Wilde concludes by asserting that sex, rather than being fundamentally about physical satisfaction or intimacy, is ultimately about power dynamics between individuals. This perspective echoes later theories, such as those proposed by Michel Foucault, that examine how sexuality is a vehicle for power relations, negotiations, and struggles within personal interactions and wider societal contexts. It suggests that through sex, individuals express, negotiate, and sometimes contest power—be it in the form of dominance, submission, vulnerability, or control.

5. The difference between sex and love is that sex relieves tension and love causes it. — Woody Allen

Woody Allen offers a witty yet profound observation on the nature of sexual relationships versus emotional connections. Allen, known for his comedic take on complex human emotions and relationships, succinctly captures a common perception of the dynamics between sex and love.

The quote invites reflection on the nature of human relationships and the different roles that sex, and love play in our search for connection and happiness. It underscores the idea that while sex might offer a temporary reprieve from life's tensions, love, with all its challenges, has the potential to enrich our lives in more meaningful and lasting ways, albeit often accompanied by its own set of anxieties and challenges.

Woody Allen is an American filmmaker, actor, and comedian whose career spans more than six decades. Allen has received many accolades, including the most nominations for the Academy Award for Best Original Screenplay.

Born: November 30, 1935

6. An intellectual is a person who has discovered something more interesting than sex. — Aldous Huxley

This quote by Aldous Huxley, offers a thought-provoking and somewhat humorous perspective on intellectualism and human curiosity. Huxley, an English writer, and philosopher known for his novels and essays on a wide range of subjects, including psychology, human behavior, and society, often explored the complexities of the human condition.

Huxley's statement is a reminder of the vast and varied landscape of human interests and the profound capacities for pleasure and fulfillment that intellectual pursuits can offer. It encourages a broad view of what it means to live a rich and engaging life, beyond the immediate gratifications of the physical world.

7. It is sexual energy which governs the structure of human feeling and thinking. — Wilhelm Reich

Wilhelm Reich, an Austrian psychoanalyst and a controversial figure in psychotherapy, made significant contributions to the understanding of the role of sexuality in psychology.

Reich argued that blockages or imbalances in the flow of sexual energy could lead to neuroses and other psychological disorders. He believed that a healthy expression of sexual energy was essential for emotional well-being and that societal norms suppressing natural sexual expression were detrimental to individual and collective mental health.

8. The tragedy is when you've got sex in the head instead of down where it belongs. — D. H. Lawrence

Lawrence observed that modern society often prioritizes intellectual understanding and rational thought at the expense of physical and emotional experiences. This quote suggests that making sexuality a matter of intellectual analysis or moral judgment, rather than experiencing it as a natural, integral part of life, is a tragic misplacement of focus. Lawrence believed that such an approach detaches individuals from their own bodily experiences and from the natural flow of life.

D.H. Lawrence's works and views, including his thoughts on the nature of sexuality, were often controversial but undeniably influential. He challenged readers to reconsider their perspectives on life, sexuality, and the connection between the body and spirit, urging a closer alignment with the natural world and our own instinctual selves.

9. Sex is more exciting on the screen and between the pages than between the sheets. — Andy Warhol

This quote, "Sex is more exciting on the screen and between the pages than between the sheets," reflects Warhol's observation of how sexuality is portrayed and perceived in media versus its reality in personal experiences

Warhol's statement suggests that the representation of sex in movies, television, and literature often amplifies its excitement and appeal, creating heightened expectations. These portrayals can be more dramatic, idealized, or intense than what individuals typically experience in their own lives, pointing to the power of media in shaping our perceptions of sex.

10. "If you need Viagra, you're probably with the wrong girl." — Donald Trump

This quote attributed to Donald Trump, "I've always said, 'If you need Viagra, you're probably with the wrong girl,'" reflects Trump's characteristic bluntness and tendency to provoke with his statements. The quote suggests a simplistic view of sexual performance and attraction, implying that the need for pharmaceutical assistance to achieve or maintain an erection is a result of being with a partner who is not sufficiently stimulating.

While the quote may reflect Trump's personal views or his tendency towards provocative statements, it is important to approach such perspectives critically, recognizing the complexities of sexual health and the value of empathy, understanding, and education in addressing these issues.

Donald John Trump is an American politician, media personality, and businessman who served as the 45th president of the United States from 2017 to 2021. Trump received a Bachelor of Science in economics from the University of Pennsylvania in 1968, and his father named him president of his real estate business in 1971.

Born: June 14, 1946 . Jamaica Hospital Medical Center, New York, NY

Special Chapter 28.

Quotes about truck drivers 🚚

Truck drivers play a crucial role in the global economy, ensuring the delivery of goods across vast distances. Their work, often characterized by long hours on the road and time away from home, demands resilience, dedication, and skill. Here are some of the best quotes about truck drivers, each followed by an explanation to delve into their deeper meanings and significance:

1."Truck drivers are the glue that holds the economy together, delivering our dreams, one mile at a time."

This quote acknowledges the essential role truck drivers play in the functioning of the economy. They are metaphorically described as "the glue" that keeps economic activities seamless, highlighting their contribution to bringing products from manufacturers to consumers. "Delivering our dreams" suggests that truck drivers enable the realization of ambitions and needs by transporting goods that fuel businesses and satisfy personal desires.

2. "The road is a truck driver's canvas, and every delivery is a masterpiece of endurance and commitment."

Here, the work of a truck driver is likened to the creation of art, with the road serving as their canvas. This analogy emphasizes the skill, perseverance, and dedication required in their profession, viewing each successful delivery as a "masterpiece" that showcases their commitment to overcoming challenges and ensuring goods reach their destination.

3. "Truck drivers don't just drive; they keep the wheels of commerce spinning and the heart of the economy beating."

This quote expands the perception of truck driving beyond the act of driving, recognizing drivers as key players in maintaining the flow of commerce and the health of the economy. It highlights their indispensable role in ensuring the continuous movement of goods, which is vital for economic stability and growth.

4. "Behind every truck driver, there's a story of sacrifice, miles of separation from loved ones, and a relentless pursuit of the horizon."

Acknowledging the personal sacrifices truck drivers make, this quote touches on the emotional toll of their work, including long periods away from family and the constant journey towards distant destinations. It paints a picture of their profession as one of dedication not just to their job but to a lifestyle that demands resilience in the face of solitude and separation.

5. "To the rest of us, it's just a road. To a truck driver, it's home."

This quote reflects on the unique relationship truck drivers have with the road, which becomes their home due to the extensive time spent traveling. It suggests a sense of belonging and familiarity that truck drivers develop with the highways and byways, contrasting the transient experience of the road for most people with the deep connection felt by those who navigate it daily.

6, "Every truck driver is a navigator at heart, charting new paths through uncharted territories with every journey."

Emphasizing the adventurous aspect of truck driving, this quote portrays drivers as explorers who continuously embark on new journeys, often through unfamiliar territories. It highlights the dynamic and unpredictable nature of their work, requiring not just physical endurance but also the mental agility to navigate and adapt to new routes and challenges.

7. "Truck drivers are the unsung heroes of the highway, delivering not just goods, but hope and progress."

his quote elevates truck drivers to the status of heroes, acknowledging their contribution not only in terms of transporting goods but also in delivering "hope and progress." It suggests that their work enables not just economic activity but also contributes to the well-being and advancement of society by ensuring that essential goods and resources reach communities.

Truck drivers' work is a testament to the interdependence of modern life, highlighting how essential their contributions are to maintaining the flow of goods, supporting the economy, and connecting communities. These quotes capture the respect, admiration, and gratitude that their hard work and dedication deserve.

Until Next Time

As you turn the final page of "Echoes of Wisdom", it is my hope that the journey through these pages has not only provided you with a source of inspiration and motivation but has also sparked a light within you that brightens even your darkest days.

The carefully curated quotes within this collection are more than mere words; they are beacons of hope, courage, and resilience that illuminate the path of self-discovery and personal growth.

In moments of doubt or despair, remember that "Echoes of Wisdom" is a companion that stands ready to lift your spirits, challenge your perceptions, and remind you of your inner strength. **Find your chapter**, read it again and let it serve as a gentle nudge to rise above the turmoil, to find beauty in the struggle, and to embrace the endless possibilities that each new day brings.

I encourage you to return to these pages whenever you seek comfort, guidance, or a reminder of your own capacity for greatness. The wisdom enclosed here is timeless, and its lessons are boundless. Whether you seek a spark of motivation, a moment of reflection, or a source of solace, this book is here to accompany you on your journey through life's ebb and flow.

May you carry the insights and inspirations from this book into your daily life, allowing them to shape your actions, influence your thoughts, and guide your path forward. And, when the weight of the world seems too heavy to bear, let "Echoes of Wisdom" be the sanctuary you turn to, a place where you can recharge, refocus, and reignite the flames of hope and determination.

Remember, the journey of personal growth and self-discovery is ongoing, and these pages are a resource that will continue to offer new meanings and insights with each reading. So, whenever you feel the need to reconnect with your inner strength or **seek a dose of motivation**, open these pages once again, and let the journey continue.

The author

As the author of "Words of Wisdom" I embark on a mission to illuminate paths with the light of understanding and compassion.

The writing, characterized by clarity, depth, and an underlying warmth, serves as a gentle guide, encouraging readers to explore the landscapes of their own lives with a renewed sense of purpose and possibility.

Beyond my role as a writer, I am a friend, walking alongside readers in their quest for clarity, resilience, and self-discovery. The words are not merely to be read but to be felt, pondered, and lived, offering solace and strength to those who seek to navigate life's challenges with grace and courage.

"Words of Wisdom" is not just a collection of quotes; it is an invitation to embark on a transformative journey with a trusted guide whose love for humanity shines through every word. The dedication of sharing the light of wisdom with the world makes this book a timeless companion for anyone in pursuit of a life lived with depth, purpose, and joy.

In closing, I leave you with a final thought: **Your potential is limitless, and your capacity for growth knows no bounds**. May this book be a guide, a friend, and a source of everlasting inspiration as you navigate the beautiful, tumultuous journey of life.

Catalin Ladaru